BE A GEO BEE

1,575 Questions for Aspiring Geography Bees

Sumhith Veda Aradhyula

Be a Geo Bee 1,575 Questions for Aspiring Geography Bees
Geozona Publishers
Tucson, Arizona
Copyright ©2015 by Sumhith Veda Aradhyula.
Cover and illustrations copyright ©2015 by Howard Yoffe.

ISBN: 0692565523
ISBN-13: 978-0692565520

Table of Contents

Preface

Hi Geo Bees!

I was a Geo Bee in elementary and middle school, and geography continues to be one of my biggest passions. Being a Geo Bee means coming up with new ways to learn more and more about the world around us. I found that a fun and effective way to do this was to set a quiz question whenever I learned a new fact or an interesting tidbit. Gradually, this ever growing compilation of questions grew into the book you now hold in your hands.

This book is a manual of geography questions and answers. The structure and format of the questions in this book are modeled upon the questions created by the National Geographic Society for the National Geography Bee. Each chapter focuses on a different topic. Within each chapter, questions get progressively more challenging.

I would like to thank Ms. Nancy Bannister for editing and proofreading this book.

Happy quizzing!
Sumhith Veda Aradhyula

How to Use this Book

This book is intended to be used as a question and answer manual. The questions and answers are in two different columns. I suggest that you use a bookmark to cover the answer column on each page. Then slide the bookmark down as you answer each question in order to check your work.

Please enjoy!
Sumhith

Question	Answer
Chapter 1. U.S. States	
Hollywood, where the U.S. film industry is concentrated, is in which state—California or New York?	California
The Aleutian islands are part of which U.S. state—Alaska or Vermont?	Alaska
Which state leads the country in peanut production—Arizona or Georgia?	Georgia
Which U.S. state is made up of an upper peninsula and a lower peninsula?	Michigan
The Canyon de Chelly (*d'shay*) monument with its famous Spider Rock, a sandstone spire that rises 800 feet from canyon floor, is in the Navajo Indian Reservation in the northeastern part of which state?	Arizona
Which present-day U.S. state was once ruled by King Kamehameha the Great?	Hawaii
The town of Hershey, located about 15 miles east of Harrisburg, is famous for chocolate manufacturing. Hershey is in which state?	Pennsylvania
Hot Springs National Park, a small national park located in the Ouachita Mountains, is in which state directly east of Oklahoma?	Arkansas
Name the Great Lake(s) that the state of Wisconsin touches.	Lake Michigan, Lake Superior
Lassen Peak, the southernmost active volcano in the Cascade Range, is in which U.S. state—Utah or California?	California
Denali National Park, which encompasses Mt. McKinley, North America's highest mountain peak, is in which state?	Alaska
Archeologists have discovered artifacts belonging to ancient Anasazi people in Utah, Arizona, New Mexico, and the southwestern parts of which other state?	Colorado
Sanibel and Captiva Islands, connected to the mainland city of Fort Myers and mainland by a causeway, are located in the Gulf of Mexico off the western coast of what state?	Florida
Acadia National Park, the only national park in the New England region, is in which state?	Maine
The Battle of Trenton that followed General George Washington's historic midnight crossing of the Delaware River in December 1776 took place in which present-day state?	New Jersey
Kenai Fjords National Park on the Kenai Peninsula, which contains the Harding Ice Field, is in which state?	Alaska
The Rocky Mountain ski resort towns of Aspen and Vail are in which state?	Colorado

Question	Answer
The Finger Lakes region, a region with 11 long narrow lakes that was once home to the Iroquois people, is in which state?	New York
The towns of Gatlinburg, Tennessee, and Cherokee in which other state constitute the main entrances to the Great Smoky Mountains National Park in the Appalachian Mountains?	North Carolina
The Sawatch Mountains, a branch of the Rocky Mountains, form part of the Continental Divide in which state that has the headwaters of the North Platte, South Platte, and Rio Grande Rivers?	Colorado
Coeur d'Alene Lake, with a namesake city next to it, is located about 25 miles east of Spokane across the border in which state?	Idaho
The islands of Martha's Vineyard and Nantucket are in which New England state?	Massachusetts
Mount Washington, the highest peak in the White Mountains, is in which New England state?	New Hampshire
Alcatraz Prison, now a historic island site operated by the National Park Service, was the first maximum-security prison in the U.S. In what state is Alcatraz Prison located?	California
Love Canal, a neighborhood near the city of Buffalo, became the subject of national and international attention following the discovery of 21,000 tons of toxic waste buried beneath it. Love Canal is located in which state?	New York
Myrtle Beach, a resort town famous for its sandy beaches and golf courses, is in which southern state with about 190 miles of Atlantic coastline?	South Carolina
Padre Island, a narrow 100-mile-long barrier island that extends south from Corpus Christi Bay in the Gulf of Mexico, is in which state?	Texas
Cape Flattery on the Olympic Peninsula is the most northwestern point in the contiguous U.S. In which state is Cape Flattery located?	Washington
Cliff dwellings constructed by the Anasazi can be found in Mesa Verde National Park in which state?	Colorado
The arid Imperial Valley, located southeast of the Salton Sea, has an agricultural-based economy that relies heavily on irrigation water from the Colorado River. The Imperial Valley is located in which U.S. state?	California
The Long Island Sound separates Long Island from which state?	Connecticut
The Canadian Province of New Brunswick shares a border with which U.S. state?	Maine
Delaware and what other state have coasts on Delaware Bay?	New Jersey

Question	Answer
Coney Island, best known for amusement parks and beaches during the early 1900s, is located in southern Brooklyn. Coney Island is in which U.S. state?	New York
Which U.S. state does not have its most populated city as the capital city—Illinois or Georgia?	Illinois
On December 17, 1903, Wilbur and Orville Wright flew the first controlled powered airplane on the sand dunes known as the Kill Devil Hills in the town of Kitty Hawk. In which state is Kitty Hawk located?	North Carolina
Which U.S. state has the largest percentage of Asian Americans?	Hawaii
Taconite, a hard flint-like sedimentary rock found in the Mesabi Range of Minnesota, is mined for what metal?	Iron
The Battle of Lexington and Concord, considered to be the first battle of the American Revolution, was fought in what present-day state?	Massachusetts
The city of Independence served as the starting point for people going west on the Santa Fe, Oregon, and California Trails. In which state is Independence?	Missouri
Considered a key turning point in the American Revolution, the Battles of Saratoga were fought in the upstate part of what present-day state?	New York
Three Mile Island in the Susquehanna River, the 1979 scene of the most serious nuclear power accident in the U.S., is in which state?	Pennsylvania
What state occupies the southern tip of the Delmarva Peninsula?	Virginia
At 17 million acres, the Tongass National Forest is the largest national forest in the U.S. This temperate rain forest is located in the southeastern part of which state?	Alaska
Merritt Island, lying between Cape Canaveral and the mainland, is in which state?	Florida
Which U.S. state changed its capital's name from Marthasville in 1845 and saw its capital city burned down by Union General William T. Sherman in 1864 during the Civil War?	Georgia
Which state, the top producer of hogs, also generates significant revenues from the production of ethanol, a biofuel made from corn?	Iowa
Saginaw Bay, an extension of Lake Huron, is in which state?	Michigan
In August 2007, a bridge collapsed and fell into the Mississippi River, killing several people in a state that touches Canada. In which state did this disaster occur?	Minnesota

Question	Answer
Name the mountains that stretch from southern Missouri to northern Arkansas and northeastern Oklahoma where Wilson Rawls' novel, *Where the Red Fern Grows*, is set.	Ozark Mountains
Name the only New England state that does not have a coast on the Atlantic Ocean.	Vermont
The San Juan Islands, which lie at the entrance to Puget Sound, are in the northwestern corner of which state?	Washington
Northern Neck, a peninsular region on the western shore of Chesapeake Bay, is bounded by the Potomac River on the north and the Rappahannock River on the south. Northern Neck, home to the birthplace of Robert Lee, is in what U.S. state?	Virginia
Michigan, Wisconsin, Illinois, and what other state have a shore on Lake Michigan?	Indiana
In terms of volume, Lake Cumberland is the largest artificial lake east of the Mississippi River in the U.S. Lake Cumberland is in which state north of Tennessee?	Kentucky
Mark Twain's boyhood community of Hannibal on the Mississippi River was used as the setting for his celebrated novels, *The Adventures of Tom Sawyer* and *The Adventures of Huckleberry Finn*. The town of Hannibal is located in which state?	Missouri
Carlsbad Caverns National Park, which is located in the Chihuahua Desert, is in which U.S. state?	New Mexico
Montauk, a surfing and artists' village on the Atlantic Ocean at the eastern tip of the Long Island, is in which state?	New York
A 600-foot-tall statue of Crazy Horse, a Sioux chief, is being carved out in the Black Hills as part of a monument in which state?	South Dakota
The *Susan Constant*, *Godspeed*, and *Discovery* are the three ships that brought the first English settlers to Jamestown. Which state's quarter coin features images of these three ships?	Virginia
The Central Valley, a large valley that stretches nearly 400 miles from north to south, is home to the most productive and diverse agriculture sector in which state?	California
Which two states touch both the Ohio and Mississippi Rivers?	Illinois and Kentucky
Aircraft manufacturing, based in the city of Wichita, is important to the economy of which state?	Kansas
Crayfish, freshwater crustaceans closely related to lobsters, are an important part of Cajun cuisine and are harvested almost exclusively in what U.S. state?	Louisiana
Cuyahoga Valley National Park, located north of the city of Akron, is in which state?	Ohio

Question	Answer
To which state would you go to visit Chambers Island in Green Bay?	Wisconsin
As a result of the Adams–Onís Treaty of 1819, the U.S. purchased from Spain portions of land that later became which present-day U.S. state with an Atlantic Coast?	Florida
Name the two states that touch both the Missouri and the Mississippi Rivers.	Iowa, Missouri
Lake Pontchartrain is the second largest saltwater lake in the U.S. This brackish body of water is located in the southeastern part of which state?	Louisiana
The Sand Hills, straddling the North Platte River, are among the most productive cattle ranching grounds of the U.S. The Sand Hills are in which midwestern state?	Nebraska
The Colorado River Aqueduct, which transports water from the Colorado River across the Mojave Desert to the east of the Santa Ana Mountains, is one of the primary sources of water for the southern parts of which state?	California
The Battle of the Little Bighorn, an armed engagement between Northern Plains Indians led by Sitting Bull and the U.S. Army led by General Custer, took place near the Bighorn River in which present-day state?	Montana
Mount Elbert, the highest peak in the Rocky Mountains and the second highest peak in 48 contiguous states, is in which state?	Colorado
The Ohio River forms the entire northern border for which state?	Kentucky
The headquarters of Starbucks, Microsoft, and Boeing are located in which Pacific coast state?	Washington
The Black Hills, a region of ridges and caverns in the Badlands, is considered sacred to Lakota Native Americans. The Black Hills area is located in western parts of which U.S. state?	South Dakota
The Bitterroot Range, a sub-range of the Rocky Mountains, runs along the border of Montana and which other state?	Idaho
The 170-mile-long Atchafalaya River, a distributary of the Red and Mississippi Rivers, is in which state?	Louisiana
Chimney Rock, a limestone formation that rises 325 feet above the prairie, served as major landmark for pioneers traveling westward on the Oregon, California, and Mormon Trails. Chimney Rock is in which present-day state?	Nebraska
Lake Placid, a village in the Adirondack Mountains and the site of the 1980 Winter Olympics, is in which U.S. state?	New York

Question	Answer
Devils Tower, a natural rock formation of volcanic origin that resembles a giant petrified tree stump, rises 1,280 feet above the valley of the Belle Fourche River in the northeastern part of which state?	Wyoming
The Getty Center, with a museum that hosts pre-20th century European art, is perched atop a Santa Monica Mountains ridge overlooking the Pacific Ocean in which state?	California
The town of Jackson, a major gateway for tourists visiting nearby Grand Teton National Park and National Elk Refuge, is in what U.S. state?	Wyoming
What state's quarter highlights images of the White Mountains and states, "Live Free or Die?"	New Hampshire
Iliamna Lake is the second largest fresh water lake located entirely in the U.S. Iliamna Lake is located north of Katmai National Park and Preserve in which state?	Alaska
St. Mary's River, which drains Lake Superior into Lake Huron, forms an international border separating which U.S. state from Ontario, Canada?	Michigan
The Klamath Mountains, sometimes called the Salmon Mountains, are in California and which other state?	Oregon
The Chisholm Trail, a historic route used by cowboys who drove cattle north from Texas to the railroad, ended at Abilene in which state?	Kansas
Two separate rivers, the Mississippi and the Pearl, form the entire north-south boundary between the state of Mississippi and which other state?	Louisiana
Pamlico Sound, the largest lagoon along the U.S. east coast, is a body of water separated from the Atlantic Ocean by the Outer Banks. In which state is Pamlico Sound?	North Carolina
Bordered by Cooperstown, Otsego Lake is considered the source of the Susquehanna River. In which state is Otsego Lake?	New York
Lake Powell, a 185-mile-long artificial lake created by the Glen Canyon Dam on the Colorado River, is spread across Arizona and what other state?	Utah
The town of Vidalia, famous for Vidalia sweet onions, is located 90 miles east of the city of Macon. What southern state named the Vidalia onion as the official state vegetable in 1990?	Georgia
The Jackson Purchase, a piece of land purchased by President Andrew Jackson in 1818 from Chickasaw Indians, is a region that is bounded by the Mississippi River to the west, the Ohio River to the north, and the Tennessee River to the east. In what present-day state is the Jackson Purchase?	Kentucky

Question	Answer
In 1988 the U.S. government chose Yucca Mountain, composed of thick volcanic rock, as the nation's first permanent underground repository for storing spent radioactive nuclear waste. In what state is the site located?	Nevada
Name the vast but shallow underground water table aquifer located mostly beneath Nebraska but extending from South Dakota to Texas.	Ogallala or High Plains Aquifer
The cities of Wheeling in the northern panhandle and Martinsburg in the eastern panhandle are in which state that was once briefly called Kanawha?	West Virginia
Which state has beaches on Narragansett Bay?	Rhode Island
Mount Mitchell, the highest point in the U.S. east of the Mississippi River, is in which Atlantic coast state?	North Carolina
The Beartooth Highway, a section of U.S. Highway 212 between Red Lodge and Cooke City, Montana, offers scenic views of the Beartooth and Absaroka Mountains and runs along Montana's border with what state?	Wyoming
Door County, which includes the Door Peninsula, has more than 250 miles of freshwater shoreline in which state?	Wisconsin
The Palouse region, a semiarid region located north of the Snake River, is a major wheat-producing area. The Palouse region is located mostly in the southeastern part of which U.S. state?	Washington
New Castle, Kent, and Sussex are the only counties in what state that borders New Jersey?	Delaware

Question	Answer
Chapter 2. U.S. Cities	
Just west of the city of Boulder are imposing slabs of sedimentary stones known as the Flatirons. The city of Boulder, where the Rocky Mountains meet the Great Plains, is in which state?	Colorado
The Research Triangle area is a region anchored by the cities of Raleigh, Durham, and Chapel Hill and is home to numerous high-tech companies and enterprises. The Research Triangle, whose population is among the most educated in the U.S., is located in which U.S. state?	North Carolina
To which U.S. city would you go to visit Independence Hall and to see the Liberty Bell?	Philadelphia
To which city would you go to see the Smithsonian Museums on the National Mall?	Washington D.C.
Most tourists visiting what city in the U.S. flock to Bourbon Street in the French Quarter?	New Orleans
With a population of less than 10,000, Montpelier is the least populated state capital in the U.S. Montpelier is in which state?	Vermont
On December 1, 1955, in protest of the segregation of whites and blacks in buses, Rosa Parks refused to get up out of her seat on a public bus to make room for a white passenger. In which Alabama city did this key event in the Civil Rights Movement take place?	Montgomery
Omaha, located on the western bank of the Missouri River, is home to Offutt Air Force Base. Omaha is the largest city in which state?	Nebraska
The international hot-air balloon fiesta that happens every October is a popular event in New Mexico's largest city. Name the city.	Albuquerque
The city of Milwaukee is on the shores of what great lake?	Lake Michigan
The first battle of the U.S. Civil War was fought on April 12, 1861, at Fort Sumter situated at the entrance to Charleston Harbor. Fort Sumter is located in which southern state?	South Carolina
Located at the confluence of the Arkansas and Little Arkansas Rivers, Wichita, one of the principle aircraft manufacturing sites in the U.S., is the largest city in which state?	Kansas
What capital city is located on a narrow strip of land between two lakes—Madison or Phoenix?	Madison
Alaska's largest city, a seaport on Cook Inlet, has more than 40 percent of the state's total population. Name this city.	Anchorage

Question	Answer
The city of Rochester, the third largest city in the state of New York, is on the southern shores of what Great Lake?	Lake Ontario
The Triangle Shirtwaist Factory Fire of 1911, which killed 146 workers and caused a great outburst against weakly enforced building code safety regulations, occurred in what major American city?	New York City
What growing state capital city in the southwest is located on the Salt River?	Phoenix
Toledo and what other city, the second largest in Ohio, are on the shores of Lake Erie?	Cleveland
Wilmington, on the Brandywine River, is the largest city in what state?	Delaware
Fargo, a large port city lying across the Red River of the North from Moorhead, Minnesota, is the largest city in which Great Plains state?	North Dakota
In 1954, the U.S. Supreme Court handed down a historic decision in the *Brown v. Board of Education* case, ruling that segregation of children by color in public schools is unconstitutional. In what northeastern Kansas city did this case originate?	Topeka
In what state are the cities of Bozeman, Missoula, and Great Falls located?	Montana
The city of Moore, located about 12 miles southeast of Will Rogers World Airport, was the site of several devastating tornadoes, including two in 1999 and 2013. The city of Moore is located in what U.S. state that borders Arkansas?	Oklahoma
What city, the largest in Maryland, is located on the Patapsco River near its mouth on Chesapeake Bay?	Baltimore
What state capital on the Cumberland River is known as Music City because it is the center of the recording industry for country and western music?	Nashville
The city of Cushing, a major trading hub for crude oil, is in which U.S. state?	Oklahoma
The city of Amarillo, which is the self-proclaimed "Helium Capital of the World," is located in a mineral-rich, cattle-ranching area in the panhandle of what state?	Texas
Sioux Falls, located on the Big Sioux River, is the largest city in which Great Plains state?	South Dakota
Each May, crowds of cheering fans fill the 1.5-mile Charlotte Motor Speedway to watch the NASCAR Sprint All-Star Race. Charlotte is the most populous city in which southern state?	North Carolina
What port city on the Delaware River, located 90 miles from the Atlantic Ocean, is one of the busiest freshwater ports in the world?	Philadelphia

Question	Answer
Hilton Head Island, which is located about 20 miles north of the mouth of the Savannah River, is a popular vacation destination. Hilton Head Island is located in which U.S. state?	South Carolina
Visitors are drawn to the twin towns of Winston and Salem for their historic plantations, which were built on the riches of tobacco and cotton farming. The twin towns of Winston and Salem, home of Wake Forest University, are located in which U.S. state?	North Carolina
The city of Lubbock, located on the Double Mountain Fork of the Brazos River near the eastern edge of the flat area known as Llano Estacado, is in the cotton-growing region of which state?	Texas
The city of Billings on the Yellowstone River serves as a gateway to Yellowstone National Park, the Crow Indian Reservation, and the Little Bighorn Battlefield National Monument. Billings is the largest city in which state?	Montana
A busy seaport on the Gulf of Mexico is Alabama's second largest city. Name this city.	Mobile
The most populated cities in the states of Maine and Oregon share the same name. Name these cities.	Portland
Marquette, the largest city in the Upper Peninsular region of the state of Michigan, is a major port city for shipping iron ore. Marquette is on the southern shores of which Great Lake?	Superior
What is the most populated city in Kansas?	Wichita
Bangor, located approximately 30 miles from Penobscot Bay up the Penobscot River, is the third most populous city in which state?	Maine
Bridgeport, at the mouth of the Pequonnock River, is the largest city in what state famous for its insurance companies?	Connecticut
Name Alabama's most populated city that lies about 90 miles north of Alabama's capital city.	Birmingham
What present-day capital city succeeded Saint Stephens, Huntsville, Cahaba, and Tuscaloosa as capital of the state and served as the site of the inauguration of Jefferson Davis as the provisional president of the Confederate States of America?	Montgomery
Name Wisconsin's most populated city that has a larger share of people claiming German ancestry than any other major city in the U.S.	Milwaukee
Newark, spelled N-E-W-A-R-K, is the most populated city in what Atlantic coast state?	New Jersey

Question	Answer
Name the port city at the western end of Lake Superior in the state of Minnesota.	Duluth
Because of its strategic location on the Mississippi River, the city of Vicksburg became a key battleground during the Civil War. In which state is the city of Vicksburg?	Mississippi
Due to its expansive and intricate canal system and popular beaches, the city of Fort Lauderdale in what state has a flourishing boating industry?	Florida
Which seaport city in Alabama is at the delta of the Tombigbee and Alabama Rivers?	Mobile
Name the most populous city in Vermont that is on the banks of Lake Champlain	Burlington
The Iditarod, an annual sled dog race in Alaska, starts near the city of Anchorage and ends in what town 1,150 miles away on the Bering Sea?	Nome

Question	Answer
Chapter 3. United States of America	
True or False—Hawaii Island is the largest island in Hawaii?	True
Which Great Lake is located entirely within the U.S.—Lake Michigan or Lake Erie?	Lake Michigan
What National Park in Wyoming would you visit to see water erupting from Old Faithful, the geyser?	Yellowstone National Park
Name the highest mountain peak in Hawaii.	Mauna Kea
Beaver Island, the largest island in Lake Michigan, belongs to which country—U.S.A. or Canada?	U.S.A.
Lake Mead and Lake Powell, the two largest artificial lakes in the U.S., were created by damming what river?	Colorado River
North America's highest waterfall bears the same name as the national park in which it is located. Name this waterfall in California.	Yosemite Falls
Name the only Great Lake that does not contribute water to Niagara Falls.	Lake Ontario
On what island is the capital city Honolulu located?	Oahu
The Niagara River, which includes Niagara Falls, connects Lake Ontario to what lake?	Lake Erie
To see Antebellum houses, elegant plantation homes built around 1830—1850, which part of the U.S. should tourists visit?	South
What hiking trail is more than 2,100 miles long and extends from the Mount Katahdin to the Springer Mountain?	Appalachian Trail
Name the island that is separated from mainland Canada by the Strait of Georgia, the Johnstone Strait, and the Queen Charlotte Strait, and from the U.S. by the Strait of Juan de Fuca.	Vancouver Island
In April 2010, an oil well had a massive leak in the Gulf of Mexico off the coast of which state that borders Mississippi?	Louisiana
Waikiki Beach, Hawaii's most visited resort area, and Diamond Head Crater are located on the most populated island of Hawaii. Name this island.	Oahu
The Transpeninsular Line separates Maryland from Delaware. On which peninsula is this line located?	Delmarva Peninsula
Breton National Wildlife Refuge, located on the Breton and Chandeleur Islands, was greatly affected by a tremendous oil spill in April 2010. Breton National Wildlife Refuge is located in what body of water?	Gulf of Mexico

Question	Answer
The headquarters of the U.S. Pacific Fleet is located at Pearl Harbor in the state of Hawaii. On which island is Pearl Harbor located?	Oahu
Name the group of about 300 small volcanic islands forming an arc in the North Pacific Ocean and extending about 1,200 miles westward from the Alaska Peninsula toward the Kamchatka Peninsula.	Aleutian Islands
Name the Pennsylvania–Maryland boundary line that is traditionally regarded as the division between the North and the South U.S.	Mason-Dixon Line
The Cumberland River, which runs through the states of Kentucky and Tennessee, flows into what tributary of the Mississippi River?	Ohio River
The Apostle Islands, in northern Wisconsin, are in what lake?	Lake Superior
The Suwannee River rises in southern Georgia and meanders in a southwestern course through Florida into the Gulf of Mexico. Name the swamp in Southern Georgia that the Suwannee River drains.	Okefenokee Swamp
Name the oil field in northern Alaska on the Beaufort Sea from which oil is transported south through the 800-mile-long Trans-Alaska Pipeline to the port of Valdez.	Prudhoe Bay
The Green, San Juan, Gunnison, and Gila Rivers are tributaries of what major river in the western U.S.?	Colorado River
Cape May, where Delaware Bay on the west meets the Atlantic Ocean on the east, is located in which state?	New Jersey
On January 9, 2014, officials discovered that a chemical used in the coal industry had leaked from storage tanks into the Elk River, a tributary of the Kanawha River. The chemical spill left more than 300,000 people without running water for several days. In which U.S. state did the chemical spill occur?	West Virginia
Name the straits that connect Lakes Michigan and Huron.	Straits of Mackinac
Name the group of Caribbean islands located about 90 miles east of Puerto Rico that are part of U.S. overseas territories.	U.S. Virgin Islands
The Susquehanna River flows into what body of water?	Chesapeake Bay
Five counties in southern Florida meet at a single point over what shallow freshwater lake that is divided among these counties?	Lake Okeechobee
The U.S. Virgin islands are part of what island group—the Greater Antilles, Leeward Islands, or Windward Islands?	Leeward Islands

Question	Answer
In one of the worst oil spills in U.S. history, the Exxon Valdez oil tanker ran aground in 1989, dumping more than 10 million gallons of oil into what body of water in Alaska?	Prince William Sound
Built during the construction of the trans-Alaska pipeline in the 1970s, the Dalton Highway travels through Atigun Pass in what mountain range as it heads north through the Arctic Circle?	Brooks Range
Ships traveling from the Gulf of Mexico to the Port of Houston go through what small bay?	Galveston Bay
What U.S. naval base in the Caribbean Sea is on land granted to the U.S. under the 1903 Cuban-American Treaty?	Guantanamo Bay
Along with the St. Clair River and the Detroit River, Lake St Clair connects Lake Huron to what Great Lake to its south?	Lake Erie
The Connecticut River, which bifurcates the state of Connecticut into two halves, flows into what body of water?	Long Island Sound
On its way to the Gulf of Mexico, the Mississippi River collects water from which tributary first—the Missouri River or the Ohio River?	Missouri River
What name did the British explorer James Cook give to the Hawaiian Islands when he first arrived in 1778?	Sandwich Islands
The islands of Saint Thomas, Saint John, Saint Croix, Water Island and several nearby smaller islands in the Caribbean Sea are collectively referred to as what?	U.S. Virgin Islands
The Grand Coulee Dam produces more electricity than any other hydroelectric facility in the U.S. The Grand Coulee Dam is on what river?	Columbia River
Manitoulin Island, the world's largest island in a freshwater lake, is in what North American lake?	Lake Huron
Isle Royale National Park is located on an island in what Great Lake?	Lake Superior
Name the body of water—an extension of the Arctic Ocean—that is bounded on the west by the De Long Strait, on the east by Point Barrow, Alaska, and on the south by the Bering Strait.	Chukchi Sea
What was the capital of Virginia before it was moved to Richmond in 1780?	Williamsburg
Mount Chamberlin is the highest mountain peak in what mountain range that stretches from west to east across northern Alaska and into Canada's Yukon Territory?	Brooks Range

Question	Answer
The Keweenaw Peninsula, site of the first American copper boom, juts into what body of freshwater?	Lake Superior
Fossils of a new species of dinosaur, the Abydosaurus, were discovered in the Cedar Mountain Formation close to Dinosaur National Monument in February 2010. In which U.S. state are the Cedar Mountain Formation and Dinosaur National Monument located?	Utah

Question	Answer
Chapter 4. Continents	
The Great Rift Valley, a massive fault line that extends about 4,000 miles north to south, is marked with numerous fresh water lakes and volcanoes. The Great Rift Valley is in which continent?	Africa
Rondador, an Andean musical instrument of hollow bamboo tubes placed side by side in order of size, is native to what continent?	South America
Nagorno-Karabakh, an enclave of Azerbaijan where the population is almost all Armenian Christian, is in what continent?	Asia
Tuareg people, nomadic tribal people of the Sahara that have been converted to Islam by Arabs, speak a Berber language and live mostly in what continent?	Africa
The yak, found on the Tibetan Plateau between the altitudes of 13,000 to 20,000 feet, is native to what continent?	Asia
The Tropic of Cancer does not pass through which continent—Asia, Europe, or North America?	Europe
Excluding Antarctica, which continent has the lowest population density?	Australia
The Maghreb was an ancient Arabic term for land in the northern parts of what continent?	Africa
The Ross and Weddell Seas can be found in which continent?	Antarctica
The Prime Meridian does not pass through which continent—Europe, Africa or Asia?	Asia
Alpaca are partially domesticated mammals kept in flocks for their wool-like fleece by native people in highlands of what continent?	South America
Vinson Massif is the highest mountain on which continent?	Antarctica
The Oromo people of Hamitic origin are from the eastern part of what continent?	Africa
In January 2009, paleontologists discovered fossilized bones of Titanoboa, a large prehistoric snake, at Cerrejón, one of the world's largest open-pit coal mines. Titanoboa is believed to have lived in the rainforests in the northeastern part of what continent?	South America
The Altay Mountains, where the headwaters of the Ob and the Irtysh are present, are located in what continent?	Asia
The Cantabrian Mountains, which extend about 300 miles east–west, are located in what continent?	Europe

Question	Answer
Which continent leads the world in wheat exports?	North America
The highest mountain peak in which continent is in the Ellsworth Mountains?	Antarctica
What continent's northwest coastal area is settled by Berber people?	Africa
Yurts are portable felt-covered dwelling structures used by nomads on the steppes of what continent?	Asia
The Svalbard Islands, with a population of about 3,500, are part of what continent?	Europe
Hausa, a Chadic language, is a lingua franca among more than 40 million people in several countries in the western parts of what continent?	Africa
The Isthmus of Tehuantepec is in which continent?	North America
Beardmore, Pine Island, and Lambert Glaciers are in which continent?	Antarctica
The Tian Shan mountain system is in which continent?	Asia
The islands of Jersey and Guernsey are in which continent?	Europe
The Danakil Desert and the Danakil Depression are in which continent?	Africa
The Sunda Islands are in which continent?	Asia
Fresh water lakes Kivu and Edward are in which continent?	Africa
Lake Vostok is in which continent?	Antarctica
With a top speed of 14 miles an hour, the Black Mamba snake is the fastest land snake in the world. The Black Mamba is native to the southeastern part of what geographically diverse continent?	Africa

Question	Answer
Chapter 5. Americas	
Iguaçu Falls, on the Iguaçu River in South America, are located at the border between Argentina and what Portuguese-speaking country?	Brazil
Name the only mainland Central American country that does not touch Pacific Ocean.	Belize
Which country leads the world in maple syrup production?	Canada
Name the only mainland central American country that does not touch Caribbean Sea.	El Salvador
Although this country ranks second in the world in terms of land area, it has the longest coastline in the world. Name this country.	Canada
The Malecón is a famous esplanade which stretches for four miles along the coast in Havana. Which Caribbean country would you visit to stroll along Havana's Malecón?	Cuba
To see Angel Falls, the highest waterfall in the world, which Spanish-speaking South American country would you visit?	Venezuela
On August 28, 2008, a strong earthquake struck at sea off Canada's Pacific coast west of the largest island in the Province of British Columbia. Name this island.	Vancouver Island
Ungava Peninsula, which consists entirely of treeless arctic tundra, is bounded by the Hudson Strait to the north and Ungava Bay to the east. Ungava Peninsula is in which country?	Canada
Which South American country has coasts on both the Pacific Ocean and the Caribbean Sea?	Colombia
The Laurentian Mountains, located north of the St. Lawrence River, are in which country?	Canada
The British Virgin Islands are in which body of water?	Caribbean Sea
What are the two main European languages spoken on the island of Hispaniola?	French and Spanish
Name the large 120-mile-long and 50-mile-wide bay, entirely in Canada, that is a northeastern arm of Lake Huron.	Georgian Bay
The largest lake in Central America is in which country?	Nicaragua
Chihuahua and Sonora are the two largest states in which country?	Mexico
A red maple leaf is on what country's flag?	Canada

Question	Answer
Roatán Island, which lies off the north coast of Honduras, is in which body of water?	Caribbean Sea
The Pacific Coast cities of Antofagasta, Valparaíso and Concepción are in what country?	Chile
Name the only two South American countries that Brazil does not touch.	Ecuador and Chile
What Central American country celebrated the centennial of its separation from Colombia in November 2003?	Panama
Which city in Canada has the most people?	Toronto
Mt. Aconcagua, the highest mountain peak in South America, is in what country?	Argentina
The Urubamba Valley, also known as the sacred valley of the Incas, is formed by the Urubamba River. The Urubamba Valley is located near the city of Cusco in what South American country?	Peru
Tiburon Island, located in the Gulf of California, is the largest island in what country?	Mexico
Which South American country has the highest proportion of people of European descent?	Argentina
Cape Chidley at the northeastern tip of the Labrador Peninsula is part of which country?	Canada
Which two countries claim the island of Tierra del Fuego?	Chile and Argentina
Venezuela touches Colombia, Brazil, and which small country to its east?	Guyana
The northern half of the Lesser Antilles Islands is collectively known as what islands?	Leeward Islands
Anne of Green Gables, a bestselling book by Canadian author Lucy Montgomery, is set in which Canadian province that lies in the Gulf of St. Lawrence?	Prince Edward Island
Port of Spain is the capital of which island country off the coast of Venezuela?	Trinidad and Tobago
Name the largest island off the west coast of the North American continent.	Vancouver Island
Name the South American country that became landlocked after losing coastal territory to Chile in the War of the Pacific in 1879.	Bolivia
The Orinoco, an important river in Venezuela, is a tributary of the Amazon River. True or False?	False

Question	Answer
Mona Passage separates Puerto Rico from this Island to its west. Name this island.	Hispaniola
Baffin Island, the largest island in Canada, is part of what Canadian territory?	Nunavut
About 26 miles off the coast of the Seward Peninsula lie the Little Diomede and Big Diomede Islands. Little Diomede belongs to the U.S. while Big Diomede belongs to which country?	Russia
Haiti and what country to its east share the island of Hispaniola in the Caribbean Sea?	the Dominican Republic
Located on the western slope of the Rocky Mountains, and adjoining Banff and Kootenay National Parks, Yoho National Park is the oldest national park in what country?	Canada
Name the desert in southern Arizona that shares its name with a Mexican state.	Sonoran
Located west of Edmonton, the Canadian national parks of Banff, Jasper, and Yoho are in which Canadian province?	Alberta
Pacaya, Fuego, and Santa Maria are active volcanoes in which part of the world—Central America, South America, or Iberia?	Central America
A vast majority of the more than 35,000 islands in the Great Lakes are within Georgian Bay. These islands belong to which country?	Canada
To which country would you go to visit the Mosquito Coast in the Americas?	Nicaragua
With a population of less than 8,000, Iqaluit earns the distinction of being the smallest Canadian capital city in terms of population. Iqaluit is the capital of what Canadian territory?	Nunavut
Lake Atitlan and Lake Izabal are the two largest natural lakes in which country that is the most populated in Central America?	Guatemala
The Grand Banks is a region where the Labrador Current mingles with the Gulf Stream Current resulting plankton rich water and thus making it one of the world's leading fishing grounds. The Grand Banks is off the coast of which country?	Canada
Kaieteur Falls, one of the highest single-drop waterfalls, is on the Potaro River in which English-speaking South American country?	Guyana
The Ona people, believed to be extinct, were expert archers who subsisted primarily by hunting guanacos, tuco-tucos, and other wild animals on what island that is separated from mainland South American by the Strait of Magellan?	Tierra del Fuego
Mount Logan, the highest peak in Canada, is located in the Saint Elias Mountains in Kluane National Park and Reserve in what Canadian Territory?	Yukon

Question	Answer
All of the land west of the Maroni River in French Guiana is claimed by what other country?	Suriname
The city of Calgary, which lies in the eastern foothills of the Canadian Rocky Mountains, hosted the 1988 Winter Olympics. Calgary is the most populous city in what Canadian province?	Alberta
Name Canada's longest river.	Mackenzie River
What is the highest volcano in continental North America?	Pico de Orizaba
At 19,347 feet above the sea level, Cotopaxi is one of the highest active volcanoes in the world. In which Andean country is Cotopaxi located?	Ecuador
The Essequibo River is the longest river in which country that borders both Venezuela and Suriname?	Guyana
In terms of surface area, which is the smallest of the five Great Lakes?	Lake Ontario
St. John's, the easternmost provincial capital city in Canada, is in which province?	Newfoundland and Labrador
Name the two countries that Lake Titicaca touches.	Peru and Bolivia
The city of Sherbrooke, which lies between the St. Lawrence River and the state of Vermont, is in which Canadian province?	Quebec
Easter Island, famous for large stone carvings called megaliths, is part of which country?	Chile
The Bay of Fundy is between New Brunswick and what other Canadian province?	Nova Scotia
The Pantanal wetland, the biggest wetland in the world, is mostly within Brazil with portions in South America's two landlocked countries. The Pantanal releases water through which river that shares its name with a country?	Paraguay River
Name South America's most populated city.	Sao Paulo
Which Canadian provincial capital city is not accessible by road from the other nine provinces?	St. John's
The sea passage that separates the Antarctic Peninsula from Tierra del Fuego is known by what name?	Drake Passage
Located about 400 miles east of the country's capital city, Pico Turquino is the highest point in which Caribbean island country?	Cuba
The Susquehanna River empties into what body of water?	Chesapeake Bay

Question	Answer
Aruba, an island in the West Indies near the Paraguaná Peninsula of Venezuela, is an integral part of what European country?	the Netherlands
The city of Fort McMurray, an oil boomtown about 35 miles west of the Saskatchewan border, is located near the Athabasca Oil Sands in which Canadian province?	Alberta
The small town of Churchill, famous for the many polar bears that move around in the autumn season, is on the shores of Hudson Bay in what Canadian prairie province?	Manitoba
The Pacific Coast resort city of Mazatlán, which lies just south of the Tropic of Cancer, is in which country?	Mexico
In which Central American country did the U.S. support guerilla fighters known as Contras that opposed the Marxist Sandinista regime during the 1980s?	Nicaragua
Which South American country has an ethnically diverse population with approximately 37 percent Asian Indians, 31 percent Creoles, and 15 percent Indonesians?	Suriname
After the creation of Nunavut Territory in Canada in 1999, a four-corners intersection was created between the Northwest Territories, Nunavut, and which two provinces?	Saskatchewan and Manitoba
Belize and what other country have beaches on Chetumal Bay, an inlet of the Caribbean Sea?	Mexico
What English-speaking country is often spared the worst effects of the region's hurricanes because its far eastern location in the West Indies in the Atlantic Ocean puts it just outside the principal hurricane zone?	Barbados
Located slightly north of the 1°30′ south latitude line, the snowcapped inactive volcano Chimborazo in the Andes Mountains has an elevation of 20,702 feet. Chimborazo's peak is the highest point in which country?	Ecuador
What country would you visit to see Tikal, the ancient ruined city of the Mayan Civilization?	Guatemala
Which country has the smallest population and the lowest population density in South America?	Suriname [French Guiana is not a country]
Iqaluit, the capital city of Canada's newest territory Nunavut, is on what large island?	Baffin Island
With abundant rains on the western slopes of the Rockies creating ideal conditions for trees to grow, what province produces almost half of Canada's timber?	British Columbia
What is the most populated island that is entirely in the Western Hemisphere?	Hispaniola

Question	Answer
Slightly more than half of the total population of Guyana is made up of descendants of workers brought by British from which part of the world?	Indian subcontinent or South Asia
Offshore oil wells in the Gulf of Campeche are an important source of revenue for which country?	Mexico
Founded by Hernán Cortés, who first landed there in 1519, the city of Veracruz is the busiest port in which country?	Mexico
The islands of Curaçao, Bonaire, Saint Eustatius, Saba and the southern half of Saint Martin Island are jointly administered by the Netherlands and are collectively known as what?	the Netherlands Antilles
The electricity produced by the Itaipu Hydroelectric Dam, one of the largest in the world, is shared by Brazil and Paraguay. Itaipu Dam produces electricity by harnessing waters of what river?	Paraná River
The Saint Pierre and Miquelon Islands, off the coast of Newfoundland, are an overseas territory of which European country?	France
In June 2010, devastating floods displaced about 200,000 people in the states of Alagoas and Pernambuco. The Atlantic Coast states of Alagoas and Pernambuco are in what country?	Brazil
Happy Valley-Goose Bay, Mount Pearl, and Conception Bay South are some of the larger towns in what Canadian province which also contains Groswater Bay and Lake Melville?	Newfoundland and Labrador
What South American country whose flag consists of three yellow, blue, and red horizontal stripes was formerly known as New Granada?	Colombia
In 1917, the U.S. bought a group of islands from Denmark for $25 million to build a naval base in the Caribbean Sea for protecting the Panama Canal. Name this island group located in the Lesser Antilles.	U.S. Virgin Islands

Question	Answer
Chapter 6. Europe	
Itar-Tass, whose headquarters are located in Moscow, is a major news agency of what country?	Russia
The Prime Meridian passes through Spain, France and what other European country?	the U.K.
To which European country would you go to hike the Snowdon, the highest mountain in Wales?	the U.K.
What is the most populated island in Europe?	Great Britain
Point Tarifa, the southernmost point in mainland Europe, is in what country—Italy, Greece or Spain?	Spain
Which southeastern European country is officially known as the Hellenic Republic?	Greece
Name the small landlocked country that lies in the Pyrenees Mountains and has borders with Spain and France.	Andorra
Akrotiri and Dhekelia are two British overseas territories that are located on a Mediterranean island. Name this island that is divided between Greece and Turkey.	Cyprus
What European island has earned the nickname of the Emerald Isle with its lush, green landscapes?	Ireland
Tourism on the Balearic Islands is an important source of revenue for Spain. The Balearic Islands are in which body of water?	Mediterranean Sea
What country, the most populous in Europe, contains eleven time zones?	Russia
The Treaty of Versailles, one of the peace treaties that ended World War I, was signed on June 28, 1919 in the famous Hall of Mirrors at the Palace of Versailles in which country?	France
The Normandy region, which was the location of a massive Allied invasion during the World War II, is in which country?	France
What is continental Europe's highest volcano?	Mt. Etna
The Algarve region, a popular tourist destination on mainland Europe, is famous for its beaches on the Atlantic Ocean. Algarve is in the southernmost part of what country on the Iberian Peninsula?	Portugal
Although Kremlin refers to the triangular fortified enclosure next to Red Square, the word is figuratively used to describe what country's government?	Russia
The strait of Messina separates what island from mainland Italy.	Sicily

Question	Answer
The tiny archipelago of the Aland Islands is an autonomous province of Finland. Most of the 27,000 people that inhibit the Alands speak Swedish. The Aland Islands are situated at the entrance to what gulf?	Gulf of Bothnia
The legendary Loch Ness, a long, narrow lake forming part of the Caledonian Canal, is a top tourist attraction in what country?	the U.K. [Scotland]
Flanders and Wallonia are two major regions in which European country?	Belgium
Praia is the capital city of what Portuguese-speaking island country off the coast of western Africa?	Cape Verde
Which one of the Central Powers of World War I was ruled by Kaiser Wilhelm?	Germany
The Costiera Amalfitana or Amalfi Coast is widely considered one of Europe's most scenic stretches of coastline with picturesque villages clinging precariously to steep sea cliffs and breathtaking rocky shoreline vistas. To which country would you go to see the Amalfi Coast's Mediterranean landscape?	Italy
With an area of more than 1.2 million square miles, Sakha, also known as Yakutia, is the largest sub-national governing body in the world. In which country is the Republic of Sakha?	Russia
The Strait of Bonifacio separates the Island of Corsica from what island to the south.	Sardinia
Liechtenstein's capital city of Vaduz is set in what mountain range?	Alps
Abkhazia is a mountainous autonomous region of Georgia. What mountain range runs along Abkhazia's northern border with Russia?	Caucasus Mountains
Crete and the Cyclades Islands belong to what country on the Mediterranean Sea?	Greece
What two languages are most widely spoken on the Mediterranean island of Cyprus?	Greek and Turkish
The Volga-Don shipping canal, which connects the Volga River and the Don River, is in which country?	Russia
The Strait of Otranto connects the Ionian Sea to which sea that lies between Italy and Croatia?	Adriatic Sea
The Douro or Duero River (ancient *Durius*), at whose delta lies the city of Oporto, is a major source of hydroelectricity for countries on what peninsula?	Iberian Peninsula
Known for its wines, the Tuscany region, bordered by the Tyrrhenian Sea to the west, is part of which European country?	Italy

Question	Answer
The Turks and Caicos Islands, separated from the Bahamas by the Caicos Passage, are a Caribbean Island Dependency of what country?	the U.K.
Rovaniemi is the capital of the Province of Lapland in what country?	Finland
The Black Forest, where the headwaters of the Danube River are located, is in the southwest corner of which country?	Germany
The Sorrentine Peninsula or Sorrento Peninsula that juts into the Tyrrhenian Sea separating the Gulf of Naples and the Gulf of Salerno, is in which country?	Italy
The Mani Peninsula, a mountainous region that is flanked by the Laconian and Messenian Gulfs is also known by its medieval name Maina. The Mani Peninsula, the home of Maniots, is in what European country?	Greece
Brittany, a rugged region with a long Atlantic coastline, ancient towns, and a distinct cultural identity, is in the northwestern part of what mainland European country?	France
President Barack Obama placed a white, long-stemmed rose on a memorial site in Buchenwald concentration camp on June 5, 2009, in what European country?	Germany
Name the small island country located about 60 miles south of Sicily in the Mediterranean Sea.	Malta
The two most populated islands in the Mediterranean Sea belong to Italy. Name these islands.	Sicily and Sardinia
Which landlocked alpine European country is divided into 26 cantons?	Switzerland
The Hebrides and Orkney Islands belong to which country?	the U.K. [Scotland]
Ben Nevis, located at the western end of the Grampian Mountains, is the highest peak in what country?	the U.K. [Scotland]
Thrace, a historical area in eastern Europe, is in present-day Turkey, Bulgaria and what other country?	Greece
Which tiny European country has a short coastline of less than three miles on the Mediterranean Sea?	Monaco
What capital city is on the Caspian Sea?	Baku
During October, 2010, highly toxic red sludge from a Hungarian aluminum factory's reservoir entered what major river and threatened an ecological disaster?	Danube River
Name the gulf that is bordered by Latvia and Estonia.	Gulf of Riga

Question	Answer
The Tokaj region, famous for wine production, is in which country immediately south of Slovakia?	Hungary
The Lombardy region, bordering the Alps to the north, is one of the major commercial and industrial regions in which country?	Italy
Name the small principality set high in the Alps astride the Rhine River and between Switzerland and Austria.	Liechtenstein
Which country, declared independent from Yugoslavia in 1991, is the northernmost of the former Yugoslav republics?	Slovenia
Name the strait that connects the English Channel to the North Sea.	Strait of Dover
Name the largest river in Europe in terms of length, discharge, and watershed.	Volga River
The Ruhr Valley, an industrial area with cities such as Essen, Bochum, and Dortmund, is in which European country?	Germany
The Baltic Sea islands of Rügen and Fehmarn are the two largest islands of what country?	Germany
Ash clouds from the Eyjafjallajökull [*eya fyatla yokul*] volcano disrupted aviation in Europe during April and May 2010. Eyjafjallajökull is in which country?	Iceland
The Minack Theatre, an open-air theatre that is situated on cliffs that jut into the Celtic Sea, is located on the Cornwall Peninsula near Land's End. What country would you visit to see a drama at the Minack Theatre?	the U.K.
The Salento Peninsula, which separates the Gulf of Taranto from the Adriatic Sea, is in the Apulia region of what country?	Italy
The mouth of Danube River is located in what country?	Romania
The central figure of the Trevi fountain is Neptune, the God of the Sea, sculpted as riding a chariot in the shape of a shell pulled by two sea horses. The Trevi fountain is in which European city?	Rome
The historic region of Karelia, bordered on the south by Lakes Ladoga and Onega, is now divided between Finland and what other country?	Russia
The Andalusian port city of Málaga, a major cultural center with an impressive array of museums and monuments, including an 11th century Moorish fortress, is in which country?	Spain
The French-speaking part of what country is known as Romande?	Switzerland
The Cambrian Mountains are in which country?	the U.K.

Question	Answer
Russia and what other country have coasts on the Sea of Azov?	Ukraine
Name the island group, an integral part of Denmark, that is located in the North Atlantic Ocean, about midway between the Shetland Islands and Iceland.	Faroe Islands
Name the body of water that lies between Greece and Anatolia.	Aegean Sea
The Battle of Waterloo, where French Emperor Napoleon Bonaparte was defeated, occurred in 1815 in what present-day country?	Belgium
The cities of Sevastopol and Yalta are located on what peninsula that jets into the Mediterranean Sea?	Crimean Peninsula
The German state of Bavaria, located in southeastern Germany, touches Austria and what other country?	Czech Republic
The Pindus Mountains, separating the regions of Thessaly and Epirus, are in which country on the Balkan Peninsula?	Greece
The Po and the Adige are the two most important rivers in the northern part of what European country?	Italy
Sylt, a German resort island in the North Sea and the largest of the North Frisian Islands, lies off the west coast of what peninsula?	Jutland
Name the largest freshwater lake in Europe.	Lake Ladoga
Name this present-day Italian port city and capital of the Campania region that is located about six miles from the volcano, Mount Vesuvius.	Naples
Transylvania, the historic plateau region of eastern Europe, is part of what present-day country with a coastline on the Black Sea?	Romania
The city of Palermo, on the northwestern coast of Sicily, is on what sea?	Tyrrhenian Sea
Most of Russia's mineral resources can be found in a region near which major mountain range?	Ural Mountains
The Dodecanese, which literally means *twelve islands*, are a group of more than 50 islands in the Aegean Sea and belong to what country?	Greece
Abkhazia is an autonomous area in the country of Georgia and borders Russia to the north. On August 25, 2008, Russia recognized Abkhazia as an independent country. Abkhazia is on the eastern shores of which sea?	Black Sea
The headwaters of the River Severn, the longest river in Great Britain, are located in what mountains in Wales?	Cambrian Mountains

Question	Answer
Much to the displeasure of mountain climbers, which country constructed a viewing platform for tourists on its highest peak, Mount Zugspitze?	Germany
The island of Elba, which is in Tuscany, lies about 30 miles east of Corsica. Elba Island, where French emperor Napoleon was briefly exiled in 1814, belongs to what present-day country?	Italy
Ships traveling from the Baltic Sea to the North Sea save about 280 nautical miles by using the Kiel Canal instead of going around what Danish Peninsula?	Jutland
After his defeat at the Battle of Waterloo, Napoleon Bonaparte was exiled to the small island of Saint Helena. Saint Helena, which is a present-day British overseas territory and one of the most remote islands in the world, is in what body of water?	Atlantic Ocean
The largest estuary in Europe (and the only place in Russia where pelicans, flamingos and lotuses may be found) is associated with the delta of what river on the Caspian Sea?	Volga River
The Peloponnisos (or Peloponnesus) Peninsula is a part of which European country?	Greece
The Marmaray, an undersea rail tunnel that connects Trakya to Anatolia, runs under what strait?	Bosporus Strait
Tenerife Island, a Spanish island, is the largest of what group of islands in the Atlantic Ocean off the coast of Morocco.	Canary Islands
Dalmatia, a mountainous strip of land where the Dinaric Alps meet the Adriatic Sea, is a region that is mostly in what county?	Croatia
The Ore Mountains are a mountain range which form a natural border between Saxony in Germany and what country?	Czech Republic
Which country that touches the North Sea would you visit to see the Utigard and the Mongefossen Falls, the two highest waterfalls in Europe?	Norway
The hot, dry dust-filled wind that blows north from the Sahara and that picks up humidity over the Mediterranean Sea before blowing over southern Europe is known by what Italian name?	Sirocco
Gotland, the largest island in the Baltic Sea, belongs to which country?	Sweden
Matterhorn Peak in the Alps, a popular tourist destination, is in the southwestern region of what country?	Switzerland
Öresund separates Sweden from what major Danish island in the Baltic Sea?	Zealand

Question	Answer
The Sea of Azov is connected to what body of water to the south by the Strait of Kerch?	Black Sea
Mount Blanc, the highest mountain peak in the Alps, is located near the border of which two countries?	France and Italy
The Chernobyl nuclear power plant, the site of a 1986 nuclear accident, is in Ukraine and only 10 miles from Ukraine's border with what country?	Belarus
The Ebro River rises near the north coast of Spain, runs parallel to the French border in an easterly direction, and flows out into the Mediterranean Sea. In what mountains, which are considered a western extension of the Pyrenees, are the headwaters of the Ebro River located?	Cantabrian Mountains
Austria and which other European country have states called Bundesländer?	Germany
The Don River, one of the major rivers of Russia, flows into what body of water that is an inlet of the Black Sea?	Sea of Azov
Name the northern Italian city situated on more than 100 islands formed by about 150 canals in the lagoon between the mouths of Po and Piave Rivers.	Venice
The Rose Valley, a region located just south of the Balkan Mountains, is famous for Kazanlak roses grown for extracting fragrant rose oil. The Rose Valley is in which country?	Bulgaria
The Dardanelles Strait separates the Anatolia region of Turkey from what peninsula in Europe?	Gallipoli

Question	Answer
Chapter 7. Africa	
Which country was known as Nyasaland when it was a British colony?	Malawi
Western Sahara, a region in northwestern Africa formerly ruled by Spain, is currently controlled by what country?	Morocco
Name this oil exporting country that is the most populated country in Africa.	Nigeria
Hafun, a small peninsula that juts out into the Indian Ocean, contains Ras Hafun, the easternmost point in mainland Africa. Ras Hafun is in which country?	Somalia
Robben Island Prison, where anti-apartheid activists were held until 1990, is off the coast of which country?	South Africa
Bloemfontein is one of the three national capitals of South Africa. Is Bloemfontein the legislative capital, administrative capital, or judicial capital?	Judicial
What mountain range stretches across Morocco, Algeria, and Tunisia?	Atlas
The formation of Eritrea as a separate country in 1993 made which country landlocked?	Ethiopia
During 2014, the Ebola virus epidemic killed more than 7,000 people in what part of the world—East Africa, Central America, or West Africa?	West Africa
Major rivers of what country rise in the uplands near the east coast and flow west to the Mozambique Channel?	Madagascar
The Great Karoo is a semi-desert plateau region which covers the southern portion of Namibia and the western portion of what other country?	South Africa
Victoria Falls, which is situated between Zambia and Zimbabwe in southern Africa, is on what river?	Zambezi River
The Cap Vert (or Cape Verde) Peninsula, forming the westernmost part of mainland Africa, is in which country?	Senegal
What is the biggest country in Africa by land area?	Algeria
The Limpopo River empties into which body of water?	Indian Ocean
The Darfur conflict has displaced more than 2.5 million people since 2003. The Darfur region, where the Darfur conflict is going on, is in which country?	Sudan
Which country was never a Portuguese colony—Cote d'Ivoire, Guinea-Bissau, or Cape Verde?	Cote d'Ivoire

Question	Answer
Lake Nasser, a reservoir created by the Aswan High Dam on the Nile River, is mostly in Egypt but extends many miles into what other country?	Sudan
The Ahaggar Mountains, a highland region in the central Sahara, are located in what country?	Algeria
What country on the Gulf of Guinea is formerly known as Dahomey?	Benin
What river along with its tributary, the Ubangi River, provides an important transport artery for river boats between Bangui and Brazzaville?	Congo River
Port Said, the northern terminus of the Suez Canal, is in what country?	Egypt
The Nairobi-Mombasa railway and road divide Tsavo National Park, famous for large numbers of elephants and black rhinoceroses, in what country?	Kenya
Name the deepest lake in Africa that is also Africa's longest.	Lake Tanganyika
Considered one of the poorest countries in the world, about 80 percent of this landlocked country is covered by the Sahara. Name this country whose biggest city, Niamey, is about 70 miles from its border with Burkina Faso.	Niger
In 2008, a small landlocked country in east-central Africa became the first country in the world to elect a national legislature in which the majority of members are women. Name this country whose national legislature meets in the city of Kigali.	Rwanda
The Casamance region, which shares borders with the country Gambia, is part of which African country?	Senegal
Table Mountain, visible to sailors 30 miles out in the Atlantic Ocean, forms a backdrop to Cape Town in what country?	South Africa
Serengeti National Park, most famous for the annual migration of hundreds of thousands of wildebeest and zebra, is in which country that is south of Kenya?	Tanzania
The city of Walvis Bay that serves as Namibia's principal port was an enclave of what country until 1994?	South Africa
To what country would you go to visit large numbers of mammals, including lions, elephants, and rhinoceroses, that are attracted to the bountiful grasslands on the floor of the Ngorongoro volcanic crater?	Tanzania
What river has the highest annual water flow in Africa?	Congo River
Masai Mara Game Park, famous for its lions, is one of the most visited parks in which East African country?	Kenya

Question	Answer
Tugela Falls, the highest in Africa, are located in Royal Natal National Park in KwaZulu-Natal Province of what country?	South Africa
Lake Assal, the lowest point in Africa and the saltiest body of water outside of Antarctica, is in which country at the entrance to the Red Sea?	Djibouti
The Caprivi Strip, a narrow band of land about 280 miles long between Angola and Botswana, gives which country access to the Zambezi River?	Namibia
The Drakensberg Mountains that extend for 700 miles from Mpumalanga Province to Eastern Cape Province are the highest mountain range in what country?	South Africa
Mount Elgon, an extinct volcano, lies on Kenya's western border with what country?	Uganda
Which country conducted many nuclear tests in the 1960s in the Algerian Sahara area?	France
Lake Turkana, Sibiloi National Park, and the Chalbi Desert are important features of which African country?	Kenya
The Mandara Mountains stretch for 125 miles along Cameroon's western border with what country?	Nigeria
Ukerewe, the largest African island in a freshwater lake, lies in the southeastern region of Lake Victoria. Ukerewe Island belongs to what country?	Tanzania
Ras ben Sakka, considered to be the northernmost point of mainland Africa, is in which country?	Tunisia
Because of the Sahara, the overwhelming majority people in Libya and what other large country to its west live in the northern part of the country near the Mediterranean coast?	Algeria
The Atbara River, a tributary of the Nile, originates in Ethiopia and flows in a northwesterly direction. In which country does the Atbara join the Nile River?	Sudan
Which African country shares borders with Angola and Mozambique?	Zambia
The kora, a stringed instrument, and the balafon, a wooden xylophone with gourds, are important instruments for the Jali music of what landlocked West African country that is named after an ancient empire?	Mali
What is the southernmost point of the continent of Africa?	Cape Agulhas
The Gulf of Aden separates Yemen from what country in the Horn of Africa?	Somalia

Question	Answer
Omar Bongo, one of the world's longest serving leaders of the 20th century, died in June 2009. President Omar Bongo ruled what oil producing central African country that was once a French colony?	Gabon
Maakhir and Puntland, autonomous areas in the Horn of Africa, are part of what country plagued by civil war?	Somalia
The mineral rich Katanga Province, whose capital is Lubumbashi, is in the southeastern part of which country?	Democratic Republic of the Congo
Which country has the largest number of Arab people in the world?	Egypt
To which country would you go to surf the shores of the Bight of Biafra—Nigeria, Liberia, or Namibia?	Nigeria
What term is used to describe the semiarid transition zone in Africa between the Sahara to the north and tropical forests to the south?	Sahel
Name the small country in central Africa whose income has increased significantly since the 1996 discovery of offshore oil in the Gulf of Guinea near Bioko Island on which the country's capital, Malabo, is located.	Equatorial Guinea
The ancient city of Timbuktu near the Niger River is in which African country?	Mali
The port city of Eyl, which in 2008 became a safe haven for sea pirates operating in and around the waters of the Gulf of Aden, is in which country?	Somalia
The Nubian Desert, a rocky sandstone plateau, is bounded by the Nile River Valley on the west. The Nubian Desert is primarily located in what country that lies south of Egypt?	Sudan
At an elevation of more than 16,750 feet, Margherita Peak in the Rwenzori Range is the third highest peak in Africa. Margherita Peak, located about 33 miles north of Lake Edward, forms part of the border between the Democratic Republic of the Congo and what other country?	Uganda
Tamanrasset, known as Fort Laperrine during French colonial times, is an oasis town in what country near its border with Niger and Mali?	Algeria
Coffee constitutes more than 70 percent of exports for what small landlocked African country bordered by Rwanda to the north?	Burundi
On December 17, 2008, the Organization of the Petroleum Exporting Countries held its meeting in the Mediterranean port city of Oran, the second largest city in what member country?	Algeria
Name the Spanish-speaking country in central Africa which consists of a mainland region called Mbini, formerly known as Rio Muni, and several islands in the Gulf of Guinea.	Equatorial Guinea

Be a Geo Bee

Question	Answer
Lake Volta, the world's largest manmade lake, was created as result of the Akosombo Dam on the Volta River. Lake Volta lies in which country on the Gulf of Guinea?	Ghana
The Chari River, an important river in central Africa, empties into what north-central African lake?	Lake Chad
What small landlocked African nation was formerly known as Basutoland?	Lesotho
Name the landlocked desert country east of Mauritania whose southern region is watered by the Niger River.	Mali
The Atlantic port city of Essaouira, which is protected from the extreme heat of the Sahara by the Atlas Mountains, is in which country?	Morocco
To better manage wildlife, Kruger National Park in northeastern South Africa was merged in 2002 with Gonarezhou National Park in Zimbabwe and Limpopo National Park in what adjoining country to form the Great Limpopo Transfrontier Park.	Mozambique
Skeleton Coast Park, a 250-mile-long and 30-mile-wide band of desolate land along the Atlantic Ocean coast, is in which country?	Namibia
Which present-day African country was formed when British- and Italian-controlled colonies gained independence and formed a single country on July 1, 1960?	Somalia
Because of the low gradient of the land, the headwaters of the White Nile and its major tributaries overflow, resulting in 30,000 square miles of swampy area called Sudd in what country?	South Sudan
The city of Ghardaïa, renowned for its coarse goat hair carpets, is located in the Mzab Valley in the northern Sahara in what country?	Algeria
The Okavango River, after flowing southward and crossing the Caprivi Strip, forms a vast marshland where it drains into the Okavango Delta in what country?	Botswana
What small African country is landlocked but has much of its southwestern border adjacent to Lake Tanganyika?	Burundi
Originally established in 1907 when the country was a German colony, Etosha National Park is home to animals that can survive in savanna and semi-desert conditions. Etosha National Park is in which present-day Atlantic Coast country that is home to the Ovambo people?	Namibia
The coastal town of Benguela was an important place for the slave trade. Benguela is in which present-day African country that formerly was a Portuguese colony?	Angola

Question	Answer
Lake Mweru, which is fed by the Luapula River, is on the border between Zambia and the Katanga Province of what large country?	Democratic Republic of the Congo
Built in 1482, St. George's Castle in Elmina served as a prison for Africans who were forced into slavery. In which former English colony bordering Cote d'Ivoire is St. George's Castle?	Ghana
The Shimahore language is spoken by the Mahorais people of what small French overseas territory in proximity to Madagascar?	Mayotte
The 14th century traveler and author Ibn Battuta was born in the city of Tangiers in what present-day North African country?	Morocco
During the transatlantic slave trade, slaves were temporarily stationed on Gorée Island before being shipped off to other countries. Gorée Island, located a mile at sea from the Dakar harbor, is in what present-day country that was once a French colony?	Senegal
Name the African country to have borders on both Lake Malawi and Lake Victoria.	Tanzania
At 436 feet below sea level, the Qattara Depression is the second deepest depression in Africa and the fourth deepest in the world. The Qattara Depression is in which Arab country?	Egypt
The Pemba Channel separates Pemba Island from the mainland portion of which East African country?	Tanzania
Ras Dashen, located about 200 miles from the Red Sea, is the highest mountain peak in what landlocked African country?	Ethiopia
The city of Omdurman is located across the Nile River from Khartoum. Omdurman is the most populous city and a commercial center in what country?	Sudan
The headwaters of three major African rivers, the Niger, Gambia, and Senegal Rivers, are located in Fouta Djallon, a highland region in West Africa. Fouta Djallon, which receives a great deal of rainfall, is in which country?	Guinea
Libya and its neighboring country have had several armed disagreements over the Aozou Strip, which contains deposits of uranium and manganese. To which country did the International Court of Justice award the Aozou Strip in 1994?	Chad
Misratah, a city at the western edge of the Gulf of Sidra, is the third largest city in which African country?	Libya

Question	Answer
Chapter 8. Asia	
Mount Fuji is an iconic symbol for what East Asian country?	Japan
The Ganges Plain, home to about 500 million people, is in which country?	India
What mountain range forms the natural boundary traditionally accepted as separating Asia and Europe?	Ural
Lumbini, the birthplace of Siddhartha Gautama, is one of the holiest places for the followers of Buddhism. Lumbini is located near the town of Kapilavastu near the Indian border in what present-day country?	Nepal
Saddam Hussein was a dictator of what Middle Eastern country whose capital is Baghdad?	Iraq
In terms of land area, what country is the world's largest landlocked country?	Kazakhstan
The Three Gorges Dam, constructed on China's longest river, is the world's largest hydroelectric river dam. On what river was the Three Gorges Dam constructed?	Yangtze River
Borobudur, a ninth century Hindu-Buddhist temple on the island of Java, is in what country?	Indonesia
Scientists were able to germinate a 2,000-year-old date palm seed found in the excavations at Masada, an ancient fortress of the Jewish people, in what present-day country?	Israel
Largely recovered from Iraq's invasion and oil field sabotage of 1990–91, this prosperous country is at the western end of Persian Gulf. Name this country.	Kuwait
Name the seasonal winds that carry moisture from the Indian Ocean to Southeast Asia.	Monsoons
Name the two countries that are both in Asia and Europe.	Turkey and Russia
The Turpan Depression is in which large Asian country?	China
The two-humped Bactrian camel is native to the Central Asian Steppes and what desert in northern China and Mongolia?	Gobi
Bangladesh has a land border with India and what other country?	Myanmar
Famous for its massive dome, the Hagia Sophia is a Byzantine church that remained as the largest cathedral in the world for many centuries. It was converted to a mosque in the 1400s and is now a museum. The Hagia Sophia is in what present-day country?	Turkey

Question	Answer
Name the large but shrinking inland sea that borders Kazakhstan and Uzbekistan.	Aral Sea
The Sundarbans, the marshy lands home to Bengal tigers, are located in West Bengal, India, and which other country?	Bangladesh
Indonesia, Malaysia, and what other small country share the island of Borneo?	Brunei
Europeans long lusted after the riches of Marco Polo's Cathay. This refers to which present-day Asian country?	China
What Middle Eastern country, known as the Hashemite Kingdom, borders both Israel and Saudi Arabia?	Jordan
Which Asian country is divided into two regions, a peninsular region and a Borneo Island region separated by the South China Sea.	Malaysia
The Kamchatka Peninsula is part of what country?	Russia
What is the present name of Singhapura, an island that the British purchased in 1819?	Singapore
Asia Minor, which may be described as a peninsula, is part of which country?	Turkey
Name the strategic mountain pass between Afghanistan and Pakistan that served as an invasion route for Alexander the Great and Tamerlane.	Khyber Pass
What country split into two in 1971 resulting in the formation of Bangladesh?	Pakistan
Mount Pinatubo, an active stratovolcano on the island of Luzon, had a massive eruption in 1991. In which country is Mount Pinatubo?	the Philippines
The historic biblical cities of Hebron, Bethlehem, and Jericho are in which present-day territory?	West Bank
The Strait of Malacca separates the island of Sumatra from what major peninsula?	Malay Peninsula
Sarawak and Sabah on the island of Borneo are the two largest states constituting about 60 percent of the land area in which Asian country?	Malaysia
Przewalski's horses, which were hunted to near extinction, can be seen roaming free in the wild forests and steppes of Hustai National Park, located in the foothills of the southern Khentii Mountain Range about 60 miles southwest of Ulaanbaatar in what country?	Mongolia

Question	Answer
In July 2007, prosecutors issued the first indictment of a Khmer Rouge leader on charges of crimes against humanity. The Khmer Rouge, led by Pol Pot, massacred about 1.5 million people or about 20 percent of the country's total population in the 1970s. The Khmer Rouge was the ruling political party of which Southeast Asian country?	Cambodia
The Mongolian Plateau is largely occupied by what desert?	Gobi
Kalimantan, a region of Indonesia, is bordered in the north by the states of Sarawak and Sabah of which country?	Malaysia
Lake Balkhash, one of the largest lakes in the world, is located in what country in Central Asia?	Kazakhstan
Sakhalin Island, separated from Hokkaido Island to its south by the Soya Strait or the Strait of La Pérouse, belongs to which country?	Russia
Which country's flag includes the yin-yang symbol and trigrams from the I-Ching?	South Korea
Rafflesia, a leafless plant with large foul smelling flowers that weigh up to 15 lbs., can be found in the rain forests of what large island south of the Malay Peninsula?	Sumatra
The Grand Canal was built 1,300 years ago and is 20 times longer than the Panama Canal. The Grand Canal connects the Yangtze River with what other major Chinese river?	Yellow River (Huang He)
Tahrir Square, a sprawling, traffic-choked plaza, became the hub of revolution which unseated President Hosni Mubarak in 2011. In which capital city is Tahrir Square?	Cairo
Mount Damavand in the Alborz Mountains is the highest peak in which country?	Iran
The sandy Kyzyl-Kum Desert, which lies between the valleys of the Syr Darya and Amu Darya Rivers, is mostly in Uzbekistan and what country to its north?	Kazakhstan
What country, a neighbor of Israel on the Mediterranean Sea, has a green cedar tree on its flag?	Lebanon
Once the center of the Ottoman Empire, this country was founded in 1923 as a secular state whose population is overwhelmingly Muslim though not Arab. Name this country that is a member of NATO and a candidate for membership in the European Union.	Turkey
In what present-day country is the ancient city of Troy, where the famous Trojan War was fought, located?	Turkey
Water from the Amu Darya River is diverted to irrigate the cotton crop in which central Asian country that borders Turkmenistan?	Uzbekistan

Question	Answer
Makassar Strait separates the Indonesian Island of Sulawesi from what island to its west that is shared by three countries?	Borneo
In July 2010, floodwaters from the Songhua River, the largest tributary of the Amur, caused destruction in Jilin Province. Jilin Province is located in the northeastern part of what country?	China
Which country conducted nuclear tests, first in 1972 and then in 1998, in a remote area near the town of Pokhran in the Jaisalmer district?	India
On May 12, 2008, an 8.0 magnitude earthquake devastated the city of Chengdu and surrounding areas in which Chinese province?	Sichuan
What country has beaches on the Black Sea, the Aegean Sea and the Mediterranean Sea?	Turkey
The annual Pushkar Camel Fair, where tens of thousands of camels are gathered, occurs every November in the town of Pushkar just outside the eastern edges of the Thar Desert in what country?	India
Built as a capital city by the greatest Mogul emperor, Akbar, in the late 1500s, Fatehpur Sikri today attracts numerous visitors for its Persian, Hindu and Muslim architectural designs. What country is Fatehpur Sikri located in?	India
Kibbutzim, cooperative communities based on collective agriculture, are common in which country along the Mediterranean Sea?	Israel
The mountainous region of the Tian Shan covers over 80 percent of the land area of what country that borders Tajikistan?	Kyrgyzstan
Manila, the capital of the Philippines, is located on what island?	Luzon
The United Arab Emirates and what other country on the Arabian Peninsula touch both the Arabian Sea and the Persian Gulf?	Oman
Bhola Island, with a population of about 1.6 million people, is the largest island of what flood prone country that borders India?	Bangladesh
What river, the longest in Syria, flows diagonally across the country and brings much needed irrigation water?	Euphrates River
The ancient city of Babylon, located between the Euphrates and Tigris Rivers, is in what present-day country?	Iraq
Plans are being made to develop the city of Gwadar into an international shipping port on the Arabian Sea. In which country is the city of Gwadar?	Pakistan

Question	Answer
In April 2009, which Asian country established its first national park in the Band-e-Amir area, a spectacular region of deep blue lakes near the Bamyan Valley?	Afghanistan
Falun Gong, which literally means the practice of the wheel of dharma, is a group that incorporates Buddhist and Taoist principles. Which Asian country has suppressed Falun Gong?	China
At over 24,500 feet, Tirich Mir and Nowshak are the highest mountain peaks in what mountain range in Asia?	Hindu Kush
The Deccan Plateau occupies the majority of the southern part of what Asian country?	India
With a population of well above two million, the city of Mashhad, near the borders of Afghanistan and Turkmenistan, is the second largest city and one of the holiest Shiite cities in which country?	Iran
Qeshm, an island in the Strait of Hormuz, is separated from the mainland of what country by the Clarence Strait?	Iran
The Ryukyu Islands that stretch southwest from the island of Kyushu to the island of Taiwan at the eastern limit of the East China Sea belong to what country?	Japan
Name the southernmost of the four major islands of Japan.	Kyushu
Buddhist monks led widespread anti-government protests in which Asian country in September, 2007?	Myanmar
Quezon City on Luzon Island is the former capital of what country?	the Philippines
Name the only national capital on the island of New Guinea.	Port Moresby
Anuradhapura and Kandy are former capitals for what island country in Asia?	Sri Lanka
With a population of about two million, Medan is the largest city on which Indonesian island?	Sumatra
The Pamirs, a highland region, occupy the eastern part of what country that is the smallest in Central Asia?	Tajikistan
In July 2010, devastating floods caused widespread damage to property and killed more than 800 people in the Khyber-Pakhtoonkwha Province of what country?	Pakistan
Negros Island, with a population of about four million, is one of the largest islands in which island country?	the Philippines

Question	Answer
Reaching 10 feet in length and more than 300 pounds in weight, Komodo dragons are the heaviest lizards on Earth. Komodo dragons have thrived in the harsh climate of the Lesser Sunda Islands for millions of years. What Southeast Asian country would you visit to see Komodo dragons in their natural habitat?	Indonesia
Name the small peninsular country that jets into the Persian Gulf.	Qatar
Name the Central Asian country and former Soviet Republic that does not touch Kazakhstan.	Tajikistan
With a population of about 200,000, Türkmenabat is the second largest city in which country that shares its northeast border with Uzbekistan?	Turkmenistan
With distinctive plants such as the dragon's blood tree, the island of Socotra boasts unique flora and fauna. Socotra Island, located about 150 miles east of the Horn of Africa, is part of what Asian country?	Yemen
The Tonlé Sap River, which changes its direction of flow twice a year, connects Southeast Asia's largest lake by the same name to the Mekong River in which country?	Cambodia
This city is famous for its ancient markets, museums, remnant Roman walls, and the eighth century Umayyad Mosque, considered one of the world's finest examples of Islamic architecture. Name this capital city that is northeast of the Sea of Galilee.	Damascus
Name the small strip of land about 24 miles long and 4 miles wide along the Mediterranean coast where people are fighting for an independent homeland.	Gaza Strip
Lakshadweep, a small archipelago whose name literally means *hundred thousand islands* in the Malayalam language, lies about 200 miles off the coast of Kerala state in the Arabian Sea. Lakshadweep is a part of which country?	India
Seget, one of the westernmost cities on the island of New Guinea, is in which country?	Indonesia
Madura Island, with a population of about 3.3 million people, is separated from the most populous island of which country by the Madura Strait?	Indonesia
Khark or Kharg Island, a small island in the Persian Gulf, has a deep-water oil terminal and is connected by a pipeline to petroleum fields on the mainland of what country?	Iran
None of the 1,200 coral islands of this archipelago country measure more than six feet above the sea level, making them vulnerable to a rise in sea levels. Name this small predominantly Muslim country that lies off the Indian subcontinent.	the Maldives
Which communist country carried out its first nuclear underground testing in 2006 near the northeastern coastal town of Kimchaek?	North Korea

Question	Answer
On October 29, 2008, an earthquake of 6.4 magnitude struck Balochistan Province in the southwestern part of which country?	Pakistan
Cebu Island is a major island of which archipelago country that was invaded by Japan during World War II?	the Philippines
Chankanai, home to one of the most popular markets in South Asia, is also one of the northernmost cities in what island country?	Sri Lanka
Ismail Samani Peak, formerly known as Communism Peak, is part of the Pamirs and is the highest mountain peak in which country?	Tajikistan
The U.S. House Foreign Relations Committee in October, 2007, passed a resolution labeling as genocide the murder of some 1.5 million Armenians during World War I. What country was allegedly responsible for the deaths?	Turkey
Lombok Island, which is separated from Bali Island by the Lombok Strait, belongs to which country?	Indonesia
The ancient city of Persepolis, founded by Darius the Great, is situated northeast of the modern city of Shiraz in what present-day country in the Middle East?	Iran
The town of Tiberias on the west coast of the Sea of Galilee is in which country?	Israel
What is the most populated island in the world?	Java
Name the archipelago of about 56 islands that stretches approximately 700 miles northeast from Hokkaido Island to the Kamchatka Peninsula.	Kuril Islands
Magnificent ruins of temples from the first century Roman city of Heliopolis can be seen today in the town of Baalbek in the Bekaa Valley. Baalbek is now the most visited tourist city in what eastern Mediterranean country?	Lebanon
On August 18, 2008, the Koshi River picked up a channel it had abandoned over 100 years ago and broke its embankment affecting more than two million people in the state of Bihar. Name one of the two countries the Koshi River flows through.	Nepal and India
Connecting the cities of Sibi and Quetta, the Bolan Pass in the Central Brahui Range has been a route for traders, invaders, and nomadic tribes between the Indian subcontinent and higher Asia for centuries. In what present-day country is the Bolan Pass located?	Pakistan
The Wakhan Corridor is a narrow strip of land in Badakhshan Province in eastern Afghanistan. The Wakhan Corridor separates what two countries?	Pakistan and Tajikistan
The ancient city of Aleppo, founded by the Hittites before 1000 BCE, is in what country on the Mediterranean Sea?	Syria

Question	Answer
The Garagum Desert, also known as the Karakum Desert, occupies about three-fourths of what country that borders Iran?	Turkmenistan
The Coromandel Coast, consisting of coastlines in the states of Tamil Nadu and Andhra Pradesh, is in which country?	India
At over 16,000 feet, Puncak Jaya is the highest mountain peak in what country?	Indonesia
Located in the northern Galilee region, Mount Meron, known as Jebel Jarmaq in Arabic, is the highest point in which Mediterranean country?	Israel
The Karakoram Highway is one of the highest paved international roads in the world. It connects which two countries?	Pakistan and China
For hundreds of years men have dug into the soft but firm tuff to create dwellings, monasteries, churches, and underground cities in the Cappadocia region. In which present-day predominantly Muslim country is Cappadocia, famous for its unique landscape where erosion has formed caves, clefts, and fairy chimneys in soft volcanic rock, located?	Turkey
Sharjah is one of the seven member states of what oil rich country in the Middle East?	UAE
Which emirate, accounting for more than 85 percent of the United Arab Emirates' total land area, has the bulk of the country's oil deposits?	Abu Dhabi
The 375-mile-long Garagum Canal supplies much needed water from the Amu Darya River to what capital city that is 15 miles from the Iranian border?	Ashgabat
The port city of Bandar Abbas, which occupies a strategic position on the northern shores of the narrow Strait of Hormuz, is in which country?	Iran
The most populated state in Pakistan shares its name with a state in India. Name this state.	Punjab
Dasht-e Kavir, a salt desert with an area of more than 21,000 square miles, has a hot arid climate and remains unexplored. Dasht-e Kavir is in the north central parts of what Middle Eastern country?	Iran
The Ustyurt Plateau, which lies between the Caspian and Aral Seas, is in Uzbekistan and what other country?	Kazakhstan
Known during the colonial era as Dalhousie Square, BBD Bagh sits at the political heart of a large metropolitan area on the Hooghly River. BBD Bagh is in what present-day Indian city that was once the seat of power during the British Raj?	Kolkata
The mouth of the Irrawaddy River is located in which country?	Myanmar

Question	Answer
To which country would you go to visit the Badshahi Mosque, the Shalimar Gardens, and the Lahore Fort?	Pakistan
The Visayas group of islands, north of Mindanao Island and separated from Borneo by the Sulu Sea, belongs to what country?	the Philippines
Name this Middle Eastern country that once was divided between a traditional north and a Marxist south until it united in 1990.	Yemen
The Maluku Islands, also known as the Moluccas or the Spice Islands, are part of what country in Asia?	Indonesia
On December 29, 2008, Koryaksky, a volcano in Russia, erupted with a 20,000-foot plume of ash, the first major eruption in 3,500 years. Koryaksky is on what peninsula?	Kamchatka
Baikonur Cosmodrome, the leading space center for the former Soviet Union that is now leased out to Russia, is in what present-day country?	Kazakhstan
What is the name of the Azerbaijani exclave that is separated from the rest of Azerbaijan by Armenia?	Naxçivan
New Britain, lying northwest of Bougainville and the Solomon Islands, belongs to what country?	Papua New Guinea
In 1998, what country conducted underground nuclear tests in the arid Chagai Hills in the southwestern part of the country?	Pakistan
Chickens were first domesticated about 6000 BCE along the Chao Phraya River in the central part of what present-day country?	Thailand
What province, located on the South China Sea, surpassed Henan and Sichuan in 2005 to become the most populous province in China?	Guangdong
The rock shelters of Bhimbetka, a UNESCO World Heritage Site, are located in the state of Madhya Pradesh and are said to hold some of the earliest evidence of human habitation. The Bhimbetka rock shelters are located in which country?	India
With a population of over five million, Selangor, whose capital is Shah Alam, is the most populated state in which Asian country?	Malaysia
In June 2010, a new species of imperial pigeon was discovered in the Foja (*fo-ya*) Mountain Range in Indonesia. The Foja Mountain Range is on what island that is also home to the Sudirman Mountain Range?	New Guinea Island
What island is separated from the Korean Peninsula by the Korean Strait, and from Japan by the island's namesake strait?	Tsushima

Question	Answer
Jengish Chokusu, which in the local language means Victory Peak, is the highest peak in the Tian Shan Mountain Range and lies on which two countries' border?	Kyrgyzstan and China
On September 1, 1983, Korean Air Lines Flight 007, on its way from Alaska to South Korea, deviated deep into Russian airspace and was shot down just west of Russia's largest Island. Name this island north of Hokkaido.	Sakhalin
Name the small Indian state in the Himalayas that is nestled between Nepal and Bhutan.	Sikkim
The eastern part of what country contains the highly mountainous Gorno-Badakhshan autonomous region, an ethnically based political subunit that occupies about 45 percent of the country's land area but has only 3 percent of the population?	Tajikistan
The Strait of Hormuz, which connects the Persian Gulf and the Gulf of Oman, is between Iran and what exclave of Oman?	Musandam Governorate
The city of Allahabad, located at the confluence of the Ganges and the Yamuna Rivers, is in the most populated state in India. Name this Indian state that has a population of over 200 million.	Uttar Pradesh

Question	Answer
Chapter 9. Oceania and Antarctica	
What is the capital of New Zealand—Wellington or Sydney?	Wellington
The Bass Strait separates which large island from mainland Australia—Tasmania or Madagascar?	Tasmania
The Barossa Valley, located about 35 miles northeast of Adelaide, is a major wine-producing region in which country?	Australia
The two main islands of New Zealand, North and South Islands, are separated by what strait?	Cook Strait
Port Augusta, Port Lincoln, and Port Pirie are cities on the southern coast of what large country in the Southern Hemisphere?	Australia
Stewart Island, which is separated from South Island by the Foveaux Strait, is part of which country in the Southern Hemisphere?	New Zealand
Which island country would you visit to travel by the *Seasider*, a tourist train that runs between Dunedin and Palmerston?	New Zealand
What is the most populated city in New Zealand?	Auckland
The Torres Strait separates Australia from what large island to its north that is shared by two countries?	New Guinea
Tongariro National Park, located on the North Island, is home to a number of Maori religious sites and to several volcanic mountains. Established in 1887, Tongariro National Park is the oldest national park in what country?	New Zealand
True or False—The U.S.A. has made a formal land claim in Antarctica.	False
The Southern Alps mountains are in which country?	New Zealand
Mt. Cook, the highest mountain peak in New Zealand, is in which mountain range?	Southern Alps
The passenger train, the *Ghan*, runs between Adelaide and what other city that is the largest in the Northern Territory?	Darwin
Lake Don Juan located at the west end of Wright Valley has a salinity level of over 40 percent and is considered to be the saltiest lake in the world. Lake Don Juan is in which continent?	Antarctica
Lake Eyre, which is normally dry with exposed salt pans, on rare occasions fills completely to become the largest lake in which country?	Australia
The Bay of Plenty and the Hauraki Gulf, which lie between 34° and 38° south latitude, are off the coast of which country?	New Zealand

Question	Answer
Which is not a Pacific Island capital—Porta Vila, Honiara, or Castries?	Castries
Auckland, Wellington, and Lower Hutt are on what island?	North Island
At 12,316 feet, Mt. Cook is the highest peak in which country?	New Zealand
What city, the second largest city in the Northern Territory, is situated near the geographic center of Australia?	Alice Springs
The 1,760-mile-long Stuart Highway extends north to south in the country's interior and connects the city of Darwin in the Northern Territory with Port Augusta in which Australian state?	South Australia
What island country in Micronesia straddled both the equator and the International Date Line until 1995—Kiribati or Fiji?	Kiribati
The International Dateline bifurcates what major Antarctic sea that bears the name of an English explorer?	Ross Sea
The sparsely populated Kimberley Plateau, with a small mining industry, is located in the northwestern region of which country?	Australia
The cities of Christchurch and Dunedin are on what island?	South Island
The two largest islands, Viti Levu and Vanua Levu, comprise about 85 percent of the land area of what Pacific island country, about half of whose population are descendants of laborers from British India?	Fiji
What city, an important transportation, manufacturing, and education center, is the largest city on New Zealand's South Island?	Christchurch
The Twelve Apostles, a collection of large natural limestone stacks standing beyond the eroding cliffs just off the shore in Port Campbell National Park, is a popular tourist attraction. The Twelve Apostles are located in which state that is the smallest Australian mainland state?	Victoria
Kakadu National Park, situated on the Van Diemen Gulf which is connected to the Timor Sea by the Dundas Strait, is home to the indigenous people of what country?	Australia
During February 2009, more than 170 people died in bush fires that gutted many towns located near the city of Melbourne in which Australian state?	Victoria
Which country conducted nuclear tests during the 1950s on the Australian Montebello Islands, located about 80 miles off the Pilbara coast of northwest Australia?	the U.K.

Question	Answer
Lake Taupo, a freshwater lake that sits in a caldera, is in an area with numerous geysers and hot springs. Water in Lake Taupo is drained by the Waikato River into the Tasman Sea. Lake Taupo is the largest lake and the Waikato River is the longest river in what island country?	New Zealand
What Australian state shares borders with all of the mainland states—South Australia, New South Wales, or Queensland?	South Australia
Name the plateau in northwestern Australia that is situated north of the Great Sandy Desert.	Kimberley Plateau
The Antarctic Peninsula separates the Bellingshausen Sea from what other sea?	Weddell Sea

Question	Answer
Chapter 10. World Cities	
The cities of Cardiff, Belfast, and Liverpool are important cities in what island country?	the U.K.
The city of Alexandria, which once had a famous lighthouse that is considered one of the seven wonders of the ancient world, is an important port city on the Mediterranean Sea in what present-day country?	Egypt
Serrekunda is the largest city in what small west African country that is surrounded on three sides by Senegal?	The Gambia
Although it is not one of the two capitals, Santa Cruz is the largest city in what South American country?	Bolivia
Thessaloníki is the second largest city in what country that hosted the 2004 Summer Olympics?	Greece
Which country does not have its most populous city as the capital city—New Zealand or Germany?	New Zealand
The South African province of Gauteng is the smaller of the two provinces that do not border any other country or ocean. Gauteng also contains South Africa's administrative capital. Name this capital city.	Pretoria
Pristina is the capital city of what country whose population is predominantly Muslim?	Kosovo
The city of Karachi on the Arabian Sea is the largest city and commercial center of which country?	Pakistan
Matadi, an important Central African port city along the Congo River, is about five miles away from the Democratic Republic of the Congo's border with what country that was a former Portuguese colony?	Angola
The city of Dijon, a shipping center for Burgundy wines produced in the surrounding areas, is in which European country?	France
With a population of about 22,500, Birkirkara is the largest city in what Mediterranean island country?	Malta
What is the former name of Ho Chi Minh City located in southern Vietnam?	Saigon
Bujumbura, the largest and busiest port on Lake Tanganyika, is in which country?	Burundi
Table Mountain, a flat topped mountain that is one of South Africa's most famous landmarks, forms a dramatic setting for the harbor of what city?	Cape Town

Question	Answer
The Schönbrunn Palace, a former royal palace built in the early 1700s, is one of the most important cultural monuments and one of the major tourist attractions in what capital city where German is the native language?	Vienna
The city of Concepción, struck by a tremendous 8.8 magnitude earthquake in February 2010, is about 270 miles southwest of what country's capital city?	Chile
The city of Brno, located in the historical region of Moravia, is the second largest city in what central European country?	Czech Republic
What former national capital, also the most populated city in Nigeria, was named by Portuguese traders after a port in Portugal?	Lagos
In which French Pacific overseas territory is Nouméa the largest city and capital?	New Caledonia
Oranjestad is the largest city and capital of what Dutch overseas territory in the Caribbean Sea?	Aruba
Iráklion is the largest city on the largest and most populous Greek island. Name this island in the Mediterranean Sea.	Crete
Al Ayn, an educational and cultural center and the fourth largest city in the United Arab Emirates, is near the country's eastern border with what other country?	Oman
What Brazilian city, a popular tourist destination, is located on the western shores of Guanabara Bay?	Rio de Janeiro
Constanta is the major seaport of what country located on the Black Sea?	Romania
The city of Dodoma, the legislative capital and the designated future national capital, about 300 miles southeast of Lake Victoria, is in what country?	Tanzania
To which country would you go to see the Salzburg Festival, an annual music festival held in the city of Salzburg, where the composer Wolfgang Amadeus Mozart was born?	Austria
Extensive rainfall over a period of three months in 2011 in the Chayo Praya and Mekong River Basins yielded extensive floods downstream resulting in the closure of the Don Mueang Airport in what Asian capital city?	Bangkok
Cotonou is the largest city in what country sandwiched in between Togo and Nigeria?	Benin
The city of Reims, founded by Gauls in 80 BC, is in the Champagne-Ardenne region of what country?	France
Outside of Europe, what are the two closest capital cities in the world?	Kinshasa and Brazzaville

Question	Answer
What is Bolivia's administrative capital—La Paz or Sucre?	La Paz
Founded in 11th century, the city of Tombouctou or Timbuktu, a trading post on the southern edge of the Sahara, is in what present-day landlocked country?	Mali
What are the two closest capital cities in the world?	Rome and Vatican City
Ko Phuket Island, an international tourist destination and home to many popular beaches, was devastated by a tsunami on December 26, 2004. Ko Phuket is what country's largest island?	Thailand
Ajaccio and Bastia are the two largest cities on which French Island?	Corsica
Iqaluit, the capital of Nunavut Territory, was known by what name before 1987?	Frobisher Bay
The cities of Cork and Galway are the second and third most populated cities in what European country?	Ireland
The city of Blantyre is the financial and commercial center in what narrow southeast African country?	Malawi
In addition to the capital city, Innsbruck, Salzburg and Graz are major cities in what European country?	Austria
The city of Benghazi on the Gulf of Sidra, a large inlet of Mediterranean Sea, is the second largest city in what country?	Libya
Many remains of Inca times can be seen in the Andean city of Cuzco or Cusco. In what present-day country is the Incan capital city of Cuzco?	Peru
The city of Seville in the Andalusia region of what country is connected to the Gulf of Cádiz by the navigable river, the Guadalquivir?	Spain
The city of Ayutthaya, located in a rich rice-producing region in Asia, has several magnificent Buddhist pagodas. Ayutthaya served as a national capital city until the Burmese invasion in the 18th century for what present-day country?	Thailand
With a majority of Pashto-speaking people, Kandahar or Qandahar, is the second largest city in what landlocked country?	Afghanistan
The Black Sea city of Varna is in which country on the Balkan Peninsula?	Bulgaria
Name the United Arab Emirates' most populous city that is also the country's chief port and commercial center.	Dubai
What city, the capital of Jalisco state, is the second most populous city of Mexico?	Guadalajara
The city of Beersheba in the Negev is in which country?	Israel

Question	Answer
Cagliari is largest city and capital of what Italian island in the Mediterranean Sea?	Sardinia
Kaohsiung, one of the world's largest ports, was the site of the World Games in 2009. Kaohsiung is the second largest city in which Asian island country?	Taiwan
The city of Arusha, located on the southern slopes of Mount Meru on the eastern edge of the Great Rift Valley, serves as a tourist gateway to Olduvai Gorge and the nation's scenic national parks. In which African country is Arusha?	Tanzania
Crufts dog show, considered to be the largest annual dog show in the world, has been run since 1886. Crufts is generally held every March at the National Exhibition Centre in the second most populous city in the U.K. Name this city.	Birmingham
Maracaibo is the second most populous city in which country—Venezuela or Brazil?	Venezuela
The European Space Operations Centre, which served as the main mission control center for the robotic space probe that landed on a comet in November 2014, is in the city of Darmstadt. The city of Darmstadt is located in the Frankfurt metropolitan region of which country?	Germany
What Chinese provincial capital city, located in southern China on the Pearl River, is formerly known as Canton—Guangzhou, Shanghai or Chengdu?	Guangzhou
Funchal is the largest city in what island territory of Portugal that is located about 550 miles southwest of the Iberian Peninsula?	Madeira Islands
Monterrey, capital of the state of Nuevo Leon, is which country's center of heavy industry including the iron and steel industry?	Mexico
The ruins of Carthage, an ancient city-state on the North African coast that was founded by Phoenicians, later became a major port and commercial power in the western Mediterranean. Carthage can be found near which present-day African capital city that is closest to Sicily?	Tunis
Potala and Norbulingka palaces, former residences of spiritual leaders, the Dalai Lamas, are in what Asian city?	Lhasa
The port city of Bergen is the second most populated city in what Scandinavian country?	Norway
The army headquarters for what Islamic country are located in the city of Rawalpindi in Punjab Province?	Pakistan
Snowcapped Mount Ararat, the tallest peak in Turkey, is easily visible from what neighboring capital city?	Yerevan
The city of Dubrovnik, located on the Dalmatian Coast of the Adriatic Sea, is a major tourist resort in what country?	Croatia

Question	Answer
Each year, hundreds of thousands of Muslim pilgrims pass through what port city on the Red Sea on their way to Mecca?	Jeddah
Which city is closest to the International Date Line—Auckland, Mumbai, or London?	Auckland
The cities of Verona and Bologna are located in the northern part of which European country?	Italy
Yaren is the de facto capital of what island country in Micronesia that is the smallest republic in the world?	Nauru
Durban and East London are seaports on the Indian Ocean in which country?	South Africa
Timber, sago, and rubber are some of the commodities exported from the port city of Kuching, capital of Sarawak state, on what body of water?	South China Sea
The Tsukiji fish market, considered the biggest wholesale fish and seafood market in the world, is a major attraction for foreign visitors to what capital city?	Tokyo
Located near important coalfields and steel-producing areas, what port city on the Clyde River grew during the Industrial Revolution to become the largest city in Scotland?	Glasgow
Chittagong, a seaport on the Bay of Bengal, is what country's second largest city and its busiest port ?	Bangladesh
Like much of the nation, the city of Bulawayo has been experiencing a steep decline in living standards in recent years. Bulawayo is the second largest city in what landlocked African country?	Zimbabwe
Known formerly as Smyrna, the city of Izmir is an important port on the Aegean Sea in what country?	Turkey
Guayaquil, the main outlet for bananas, cacao, and other exports through its Pacific Ocean port, has evolved into the largest city and the leading economic center for which South American country?	Ecuador
Name the city about 170 miles northwest of Shanghai on the Yangtze River that served sporadically as the national capital of China from the third century until 1949.	Nanjing
Arequipa, a major city whose chief industry is the grading and packing of alpaca wool, sits in the Andes at 7,800 feet above sea level in the southern part of which country?	Peru
Makassar is the largest city on what Indonesian Island?	Sulawesi

Question	Answer
With a population of about three million people, Douala is the largest city in which African country whose flag consists of three vertical green, red, and yellow stripes, and a yellow star in the center?	Cameroon
During the colonial period, Haiphong served as France's main naval base in mainland Asia. Today, Haiphong is the third largest city and one of the most important port cities in what country?	Vietnam
Genoa and Gioia Tauro are important port cities in what Mediterranean country?	Italy
Spandau Prison, which housed some of the most infamous Nazi war criminals from the Nuremberg Trials, was demolished in 1987 to prevent it from becoming a neo-Nazi shrine. Spandau Prison was located in what capital city?	Berlin
Topkapi Palace, Dolmabahce Palace and Yildiz Palace, which were homes to powerful sultans that once ruled the Ottoman Empire, are in what large city?	Istanbul
In November 2013, Super Typhoon Haiyan devastated the city of Tacloban on Cancabato Bay on Leyte Island. The city of Tacloban is located in which Asian country?	the Philippines
On September 30, 2009, a 7.6 magnitude earthquake hit about 31 miles off the coast of Padang, killing more than 770 people. Padang is a port city on the Indian Ocean in which country?	Indonesia
Which is not a port city on the Gulf of Guinea—Accra, Abuja, or Lomé?	Abuja

Question	Answer
Chapter 11. Rivers as Borders: United States	
What river forms the entire border between Iowa and Wisconsin?	Mississippi River
What river do you cross to enter California from Arizona?	Colorado River
What river rises on the western slopes of the Catskill Mountains and forms the boundary between Pennsylvania and New Jersey?	Delaware River
The Astoria Bridge, connecting the towns of Astoria, Oregon, to Megler, Washington, spans what river?	Columbia River
What river forms the entire border between the states of West Virginia and Ohio?	Ohio River
What river runs along the entire boundary between the states of Arkansas and Tennessee?	Mississippi River
Name the river that forms the boundary between Vermont and New Hampshire.	Connecticut River
What river constitutes most of the boundary between Georgia and South Carolina before it empties into the Atlantic Ocean?	Savannah River
What river winds south through Grand Teton National Park, flows westward into Idaho, and then forms part of Idaho's border with Oregon before it empties into the Columbia River?	Snake River
Two separate rivers, the Mississippi and Pearl Rivers, form the entire north-south boundary between Mississippi State and what other state?	Louisiana
What river, a tributary of the Mississippi River, forms part of the border between Texas and Oklahoma?	Red River
The Des Moines River rises in southwestern Minnesota, flows about 525 miles in a southeasterly direction, and joins the Mississippi River. For about 25 miles above its mouth, the Des Moines River serves as the boundary between Missouri and what other state?	Iowa
The Menominee River, named for the tribes who once lived in this area, forms the eastern part of the border between Michigan's Upper Peninsula and what state?	Wisconsin
The 550-mile-long Sabine River, in its lower course, forms part of the boundary between Texas and what other state before the river empties into the Gulf of Mexico?	Louisiana
The Big Sandy River and its tributary the Tug Fork River form West Virginia's short border with which state to its west?	Kentucky

Question	Answer
The St. Marys River in the southeastern U.S. drains Okefenokee Swamp to the Atlantic Ocean. The St. Marys River forms part of the boundary between which two states?	Georgia and Florida
The Mississippi River and its tributary the St. Croix River form the border between Wisconsin and which other state?	Minnesota
The Poultney River meanders for 40 miles through several towns and scenic areas before it drains into the southern extent of Lake Champlain. The Poultney River defines a portion of the border between New York and which other state?	Vermont
What river forms part of the boundary between West Virginia and Maryland and also separates Virginia from Maryland?	Potomac River
The Ohio River separates the state of Kentucky from Ohio and what other states to Kentucky's north?	Indiana and Illinois
The Perdido River forms the entire east-west border between Florida's panhandle and what other state?	Alabama
The Mississippi River demarks the short 50-mile-long border between Kentucky and what other state?	Missouri
The Wabash River, a tributary of the Ohio River, starts in Indiana and forms part of the border between Indiana and what other state?	Illinois
The Chattahoochee River forms part of the boundary between Alabama and which other state to its east?	Georgia
What river that empties into Lake Winnipeg forms most of the borders between North Dakota and Minnesota?	Red River of the North

Question	Answer
Chapter 12. Rivers as Borders: World	
The St. Lawrence River forms part of the border between which two countries in North America?	U.S.A. and Canada
What river forms the border between the state of Texas and Mexico?	Rio Grande River
The Tekeze Wenz River forms part of the border between Eritrea and what other country from which it gained independence in 1993?	Ethiopia
The Cuyuní River forms part of the border between Venezuela and what other country to its east?	Guyana
The Hondo River and its tributary the Azul River form nearly all of Mexico's entire border with what country?	Belize
The San Juan River forms part of Nicaragua's southern border with what country?	Costa Rica
The Cuando River forms part of Zambia's western border with which other country?	Angola
The Neman or Nieman River is a major Eastern European river arising in Belarus and flowing through Lithuania before draining into the Baltic Sea. The Neman River forms the border between Lithuania and a Russian exclave to its west. Name this Russian exclave.	Kaliningrad Oblast
People trying to escape hyperinflation and unemployment in Zimbabwe are seen crossing Limpopo River to enter which country?	South Africa
The 700-mile-long Harirud River, which disappears in the steppe region south of the Garagum Desert, forms part of the Boundary between Turkmenistan and what other country?	Iran
The Cunene and Cubango Rivers form part of the boundary between Angola and which country to its south?	Namibia
The Kasai River, a tributary of the Congo River, forms part of the boundary between the Democratic Republic of the Congo and what other country that is a former Portuguese colony?	Angola
The Mono River is the principal river of Togo and forms part of Togo's boundary with which other country to its east?	Benin
The Sarstun River which flows into the Gulf of Honduras forms Belize's southern border with what country?	Guatemala
With its headwaters in the foothills of the Andes Cordillera in Bolivia, what river forms the border between Argentina and Paraguay before it joins the Paraguay River?	Pilcomayo River

Question	Answer
The Unity Bridge, being built across the Ruvuma River in East Africa will connect Tanzania and what other country?	Mozambique
The cities of Brownsville and Matamoros in North America are connected by two bridges across what river?	Rio Grande River
The Sava River forms part of the north-south border between Bosnia and Herzegovina and what country to its north?	Croatia
What river forms much of the northern border of Bulgaria?	Danube River
The Oder River, which starts in northeastern Czech Republic, forms the boundary between what two countries before it empties into the Baltic Sea?	Germany and Poland
The Senegal River, which flows into Atlantic Ocean, forms the entire border between Senegal and which other country to its north?	Mauritania
The Karun River, the only navigable river in Iran, is a tributary of what river that forms part of the border between Iran and Iraq?	Shatt al Arab River
Two friendship bridges across the Mekong River connect Laos to what country to its west?	Thailand
The Cavally River flowing south from its source in Guinea forms much of the border between Liberia and which other country to its east?	Côte d'Ivoire
What river forms part of the international border between South Africa and Namibia?	Orange River
The Morava River, which starts near the border between Poland and the Czech Republic, forms much of the border between Austria and what other country before joining the Danube River?	Slovakia
The Ubangi River, the longest tributary of the Congo River, forms part of the border between the Democratic Republic of the Congo and what landlocked country?	Central African Republic
The Salween River, which forms part of the border between China and Myanmar as well as part of the border between Thailand and Myanmar, empties into what arm of the Andaman Sea?	Gulf of Martaban

Question	Answer
Chapter 13. Rivers and Nearby Cities	
Name the European capital city that is on the Thames River.	London
Jefferson City, a midwestern U.S. state capital, is on what river?	Missouri River
Which European river has the most capital cities on it?	Danube River
The capital city of Egypt is on the world's longest river. Name this river.	Nile River
Karachi, the biggest city in Pakistan, is in the delta of which river?	Indus River
The city of Portland, Oregon, lies at the confluence of what two rivers?	Columbia and Willamette Rivers
Varanasi, a holy place for Hindus, is on what river?	Ganges River
The city of Passau is known as the City of Three Rivers because it is located at the confluence of the Danube, Inn, and Ilz Rivers. In June 2013, Passau suffered the worst flooding in 500 years that affected many areas in Bavaria. The city of Passau is located in what country?	Germany
Shanghai, the most populous city in China, is at the mouth of what river?	Yangtze River
Which former capital city—Vietnam's largest city and financial hub—is in the delta of the Mekong River?	Ho Chi Minh City
To see the Fabricius Bridge, one of the oldest bridges that is still in use on the Tiber River, to which city will you go?	Rome
What city in Croatia is situated on the Sava River on the southern slopes of the Medvednica Mountains?	Zagreb
In May 2010, what river caused tremendous floods in Nashville, Tennessee, resulting in extreme damage to property?	Cumberland River
What South American capital city lies near the confluence of the Paraguay and Pilcomayo Rivers?	Asunción
What capital city near Incheon International Airport on Korean Peninsula is on the banks of Han River?	Seoul
The city of Belgrade in Serbia is at the confluence of the Sava and what other river?	Danube River
The city of Guwahati in the northeastern Indian state of Assam is on the banks of which major river that joins the Ganges River in Bangladesh?	Brahmaputra River
The cities of Knoxville and Chattanooga in Tennessee and Huntsville in Alabama are on what river?	Tennessee River

Question	Answer
The Mekong River, the most important river in southeastern Asia, has two capital cities on its banks. Name one of them.	Vientiane, Phnom Penh
What city in the state of Ohio is located at the mouth of the Cuyahoga River?	Cleveland
Name the Italian city located on the Arno River, known as the Cradle of the Renaissance, and filled with architectural jewels including the domed cathedral, Santa Maria del Fiore.	Florence
The city of Dresden, capital of the German state of Saxony, is on the banks of what river?	Elbe River
What river provides a transportation link between Niamey and Bamako?	Niger River
The City of Basel in northern Switzerland is on the banks of what major river?	Rhine River
Bangui, the capital of the Central African Republic, is on the banks of what river that is a chief tributary of the Congo River	Ubangi River

Question	Answer
Chapter 14. Bodies of Water	
Which body of water is in Utah—the Great Salt Lake or Lake Erie?	Great Salt Lake
Which lake is entirely in Canada—Great Bear Lake or Lake Superior?	Great Bear Lake
The world's deepest lake, which accounts for one-fifth of the world's freshwater reserves, is threatened by massive pollution. Name this Siberian lake.	Lake Baikal
Sable Island, located about 190 miles southeast of Nova Scotia, is renowned for its wild horses and shipwrecks. Sable Island is located in what ocean?	Atlantic Ocean
Name the river that rises in the Black Forest of Germany and empties into the Black Sea.	Danube River
The city of Freetown was founded in 1792 as a land for freed African American slaves. Today, the city of Freetown is the largest city and the principal port of Sierra Leone. Freetown is a port city on what ocean?	Atlantic Ocean
The Isle of Man, an island belonging to the U.K., is in what sea?	Irish Sea
The Bab al Mandeb or Strait of Tears connects the Gulf of Aden to what body of water?	Red Sea
The Gulf of Anadyr, an arm of the Bering Sea, is in the Republic of Chukotka in what country?	Russia
The Gulf of Lion, on which the port city of Marseille lies, is an extension of the Mediterranean Sea. The Gulf of Lion is in what country?	France
Starting near Somalia's border with Ethiopia, the Jubba River flows south into what ocean?	Indian Ocean
During the summer of 2014, nearly half a million residents of Toledo, Ohio, had to shut off tap water because of toxins caused by a massive algae bloom in the nearby lake that is the source of drinking water. What Great Lake is the source of drinking water for the residents of Toledo?	Lake Erie
At the confluence of the Blue and White Niles in Africa lies Tuti Island, which is responsible for a large portion of what country's produce supply?	Sudan
The South African city of Durban in KwaZulu-Natal state is a major port on what large body of water?	Indian Ocean
The Vaal River, a tributary of the Orange River, is in which African country?	South Africa
The Huang He River flows in to the Bohai Sea, an arm of what other sea?	Yellow Sea

Question	Answer
Malebo Pool, formerly known as Stanley Pool, contains the Île Mbamou. Malebo Pool is a shallow lake-like widening in the lower reaches of what river?	Congo River
The Gulf of Mannar separates India from what country?	Sri Lanka
The Uélé River, a tributary flowing west into the Ubangi River, is in what country?	The Democratic Republic of the Congo
The Yangtze River flows from the mountains of Tibet and empties into what body of water?	East China Sea
The Strait of Tiran, connecting the Gulf of Aqaba with the Red Sea, is controlled by which two countries?	Saudi Arabia and Egypt
The Shatt al Arab River flows from the confluence of what two major rivers?	Tigris and Euphrates Rivers
The waters of Lake Peipus are shared between Russia and what Baltic state?	Estonia
The Chu River, starting at the confluence of the Dzhuvanaryk and Kochkor Rivers in the Tian Shan Mountains, spans Kyrgyzstan and what other country to its northwest?	Kazakhstan
The Ishim River, a tributary of the Irtysh River, has its source in the northeast parts of what country?	Kazakhstan
Mamadou Tandja was elected president after a coup in 1999 in what landlocked West African country that is 95 percent Muslim and has a border on Lake Chad?	Niger
La Pérouse Strait, separating the Russian Sakhalin Island from the Japanese Hokkaido Island, connects which two bodies of water?	Sea of Okhotsk and Sea of Japan
Joseph Bonaparte Gulf, bordering the Australian state of Western Australia and the Northern Territory of Australia, is an arm of what sea?	Timor Sea
Lake Albert, part of the Nile River system, is sandwiched between the Democratic Republic of the Congo and what other country?	Uganda
Qoraqalpoghiston or Karakalpakstan, an autonomous republic constituting the western third of Uzbekistan, has what large body of water as part of its northern border?	Aral Sea
Lake Prespa in southwestern Macedonia borders which two other countries in the Balkan Peninsula?	Greece and Albania
Keban and Ataturk Dams in Turkey and Tabqa Dam in Syria reduce water flows of what important river in West Asia before the river enters Iraq?	Euphrates River

Question	Answer
Issyk Kul, located in the Tian Shan Mountains, is the second largest saltwater lake in the world. Issyk Kul is in the northeastern part of which country?	Kyrgyzstan
Lake Scutari, the largest lake in the Balkan Peninsula, is shared between Albania and which country to its northwest?	Montenegro
Mayotte, a French overseas territory located just north of 13° N latitude, is in which channel?	Mozambique Channel
What North Atlantic sea, famous for its aquatic life, is the only sea in the world to be bordered by ocean currents rather than by land?	Sargasso Sea
The Bhagirathi and Alaknanda Rivers are the two important headstreams of what holy river in northern India?	Ganges River
Lake Kariba, created by the Kariba Dam, is the world's largest manmade lake by volume of water. Lake Kariba was created by damming which African river?	Zambezi River
The Song Hong River, also known as the Red River, flows through the city of Hanoi and empties into what body of water?	Gulf of Tonkin
Lake Saimaa, the fourth largest lake in Europe, is in what country that fought the Winter War against Russia during 1939–1940?	Finland
Name the gulf on which Egypt, Israel, and Jordan have coastlines.	Gulf of Aqaba
The Han River of South Korea flows generally westward and joins the Imjin River before emptying into body of water?	Yellow Sea
The Gulf of Iskenderun, an inlet of the Mediterranean Sea, borders the Adana and Hatay Provinces of what country?	Turkey
The Alboran Sea is the westernmost extension of what larger sea?	Mediterranean Sea
Before they were heavily dammed and water diverted for agricultural use, the Amu Darya and Syr Darya Rivers used to provide a constant supply of fresh water to what inland sea?	Aral Sea
Diego Garcia, a coral island administered by the U.K., is the site of a U.S. naval facility. Diego Garcia Island is in which ocean?	Indian Ocean
What country has beaches on the Bay of Pomerania and the Bay of Gdansk, both of which are extensions of the Baltic Sea?	Poland
Sakhalin Island is separated from mainland Russia by which strait that also connects the Sea of Japan to the Sea of Okhotsk?	Tatar Strait

Question	Answer
The island of Newfoundland is separated from mainland Canada by which strait that means "Beautiful Island" in French?	Belle Isle Strait
The Lena River flows into which sea that is separated from the East Siberian Sea by the New Siberian Islands?	Laptev Sea
Khamsin, Lodos, Bora, and Marin are winds that blow over what sea?	Mediterranean
The Palk Strait, incompletely separated from the Gulf of Mannar by a group of small limestone shoals collectively known as Adam's Bridge, separates which two countries?	India and Sri Lanka
Located between the Yorke and Eyre Peninsulas, Spencer Gulf is off the coast of which Australian state?	South Australia
In 1984, in the vicinity of Lake Turkana, paleoanthropologists discovered "Turkana Boy," a nearly complete skeleton dating back 1.6 million years. Lake Turkana, the largest salt lake in Africa, is mostly in what country?	Kenya
Honshu and Hokkaido, the two largest islands in the Japanese Archipelago, are separated by what strait that directly connects the Sea of Japan to the Pacific Ocean?	Tsugaru Strait
Name the strait between the Sinai and Arabian Peninsulas that links the Gulf of Aqaba to the Red Sea	Strait of Tiran
The Pechora Sea, into which its namesake river flows, is an arm of what sea?	Barents Sea
The Matochkin Strait, which is covered by ice most of the year, connects which two seas?	Kara and Barents Seas
With perfect white sand beaches, emerald-turquoise lagoons, and beautiful reefs, the French Polynesian island of Bora Bora is considered to be one of the most strikingly beautiful islands in the world. Bora Bora Island is located in what ocean?	Pacific

Question	Answer

Chapter 15. Cultural Geography: Festivals

Question	Answer
Which U.S. city on the Mississippi River is famous for its Mardi Gras Carnival during February and March?	New Orleans
The Calgary Stampede, an annual rodeo festival held every July, attracts over one million visitors a year. What North American country would you visit to see the Calgary Stampede?	Canada
Although the entire country celebrates Día de los Muertos, Day of the Dead, on November 1st and 2nd each year, many tourists flock to the southern cities of Veracruz and Oaxaca to witness the festival in what country?	Mexico
The weeklong Folklorama festival that celebrates various ethnic cultures in the city of Winnipeg attracts about half a million people every year to which Canadian province?	Manitoba
The annual spring time festival of Holi, where people douse one another in colors, is celebrated in the Hindi-speaking belt of what country?	India
Known as Diwali in India, Tihar, a festival of lights, is celebrated in what landlocked Hindu country?	Nepal
The Gilroy Garlic Festival, one of the largest food festivals in the U.S., is held annually in the town of Gilroy, located about 16 miles south of San Jose. Which Pacific coast U.S. state would you visit to participate in the Gilroy Garlic Festival?	California
The seven day festival of Kwanzaa is observed in the U.S. to celebrate and preserve the traditions of what heritage—Jewish, African-American, or Irish?	African-American
To witness Reggae Sumfest, a concert festival taking place each year in mid July in Montego Bay, which Caribbean country south of Cuba would you visit?	Jamaica
La Tomatina, a festival where thousands of participants throw overripe tomatoes at one another, is an organized annual food fight in the town of Buñol, about 25 miles west of the city of Valencia. To which country in southern Europe would you go to participate in La Tomatina?	Spain
To participate in Crop Over, a popular summer celebration that started more than 200 years ago to mark the end of yearly sugarcane harvest, one can go to Bridgetown in what Caribbean country?	Barbados
To which Asian country would you go to see Bonn Om Tuk, a festival celebrated in Phnom Penh with fireworks and boat races on the Tonle Sap River?	Cambodia
The Cannes Film Festival, one of the most prestigious film festivals in the world, is held annually in the city of Cannes on the Côte d'Azur. To which Mediterranean country would you go to witness the Cannes Film Festival?	France

Question	Answer
Chuseok is a harvest festival celebrated in late September or early October. During this festival, people visit their ancestral hometown and share traditional foods such as songpyeon. Chuseok is one of the most important holidays on what Asian peninsula?	Korean Peninsula
Pamplona, the capital of the Navarra region, celebrates the famous Fiesta de San Fermín each July by running bulls through the streets to the bullring and with bullfights, fireworks, and singing contests. To which country will you travel to watch the Fiesta de San Fermín?	Spain
During Junkanoo, a national festival celebrated on December 26, colorful and boisterous parades flood the streets of Nassau in what country?	the Bahamas
What country would you visit to see Naadam, a spectacular annual event of traditional sporting contests in Ulaanbaatar and the vast grassy steppes around the city?	Mongolia
Eisteddfod is a national music and poetry festival held in the summer. Eisteddfod is a tradition in what political unit of the U.K.?	Wales
The Ati-Atihan Festival, where celebrants paint their faces with black soot and wear bright, outlandish costumes as they dance, is held annually in January on Panay Island in which Asian Catholic country?	the Philippines
Tourists can wear masks and devil suits and participate in La Diablada, a carnival celebrated on the Saturday before Ash Wednesday, in the city of Oruro in the Altiplano region of what country?	Bolivia
What Latin American country would you visit to see movies in the Cartagena Film Festival held annually in the port city of Cartagena?	Colombia
People celebrating Nowruz, a springtime new year celebration, set up a traditional table setting called Haft Sin. What country would you visit to witness Nowruz festivities in the cities of Esfahan and Tabriz?	Iran
The World Roma Festival showcases Romani culture and is held annually in the last week of May. Thousands of tourists flock to which European capital city on the Vltava River to see colorful street performers, concerts. and exhibitions during the World Roma Festival?	Prague
What country would you visit to see the richly decorated elephants participating in the Esala Perahera Buddhist festival in the city of Kandy?	Sri Lanka
To which Latin American country would you go to participate in Easter festivities and watch colorful processions in the colonial city of Popayán?	Colombia
During July of each year, the small city of Viljandi, located about 60 miles west of Lake Peipus, gets swamped with visitors enjoying the Viljandi Folk Music Festival. What country would you visit to participate in this festival that celebrates European folk music?	Estonia

Question	Answer
Chapter 16. Cultural Geography: Food	
Guacamole, a dish made from avocados and often served with tortilla chips or as a relish on other foods, is common in what country that shares borders with the U.S.?	Mexico
Hummus is a dip or spread made from cooked mashed chickpeas blended with olive oil, lemon juice, tahini, and garlic. Hummus is a popular food item in what part of Asia?	Middle East
Ceviche, a citrus marinated seafood appetizer, is popular in what part of the world—Latin America or the Middle East?	Latin America
Poutine is a French-Canadian dish consisting of french fries topped with cheese curds and hot gravy. Poutine originated in what Canadian province during the 1950s?	Quebec
Kabuli Palau, consisting of steamed rice with lentils, raisins, carrots and lamb, is a traditional dish in what landlocked Asian country?	Afghanistan
Falafel is a fried ball or patty made from spiced fava beans and/or chickpeas. Falafel is a popular form of fast food in which part of Asia?	Middle East
Hangi [pronounced *hungee*] is an ancient Maori method of cooking food using super heated rocks buried in the ground in a pit oven. In which developed country can you find restaurants serving Hangi food along with Maori music?	New Zealand
What grain is the staple food for people in Bangladesh?	Rice
Paella, a dish made with rice, meat, seafood, beans, and vegetables, originated in the Valencia region on the Mediterranean Sea. People from which European country consider paella as their national dish?	Spain
Tabbouleh is a Middle Eastern salad made of bulgur wheat, herbs and spices. Tabbouleh is widely recognized to have originated in Syria and what eastern Mediterranean country?	Lebanon
Production of turron, a traditional confection made of toasted almonds, honey, sugar, and eggs, is the mainstay of the economy of the town of Jijona in the Valencia region of which country?	Spain
Raking of fish, a fermentation method for preserving fish, has been known to the Norse people for thousands of years. The word "rak" comes from "rakr" in the Norse language, meaning moist or soaked. Today, rakfisk, a dish with a very strong odor, is a unique food specialty of what oil-producing country?	Norway
Nacatamal, vigorón, and mondongo are typical dishes in the cuisine of what country that lies between Honduras and Costa Rica?	Nicaragua

Question	Answer
A chuchito, which literally means little dog in Spanish, resembles a Mexican tamale. Chuchitos are native to the cuisine of what Central American country that borders Mexico?	Guatemala
For centuries, fish caught in the Tigris River have been used in this country to prepare masgouf, a dish made by grilling a whole fish. Name this oil-exporting country where masgouf is a traditional dish.	Iraq
Mohinga, a thickened fish soup with rice vermicelli, is a very popular breakfast dish in the cities of Mandalay and Naypyidaw. Mohinga is considered as the national dish of what country?	Myanmar
Scones are biscuits often served with jam or clotted cream at teatime in what European country?	the U.K.
Doogh is a Persian yogurt drink flavored with salt and dried mint and sometimes made with carbonated mineral water. In which Middle Eastern country is doogh a popular drink?	Iran
Goulash, a stew made with beef, potatoes, onions, and paprika seasoning, and gombutz, a dish made with cabbage, rice, ground meat, and tomatoes, are typical foods from what eastern European country?	Hungary
Pierogi [*pee-row-gee*], dumplings containing cream cheese and potatoes, are popular in what country that borders the Kaliningrad Oblast of Russia?	Poland
Roquefort cheese, produced with techniques developed in 11th century, is aged for more than three months in the limestone caves of Combalou near the city of Toulouse. Authentic roquefort cheese is a product of what country?	France
Traditional restaurants in cities such as Nagoya, Sapporo, and Kobe offer oshibori, a hot wet towel to clean one's hands before eating. Oshibori is a common sight in the restaurants of what country?	Japan
Halo-Halo, a colorful dessert snack consisting of milk, sweet beans, fruits, and a layer of shaved ice, is popular among the people of Quezon City on what island in the Philippines?	Luzon
Shumlay, a drink made of yogurt, honey, and spices, is a traditional drink of the Pashtuns in which landlocked Asian country that borders Iran.	Afghanistan
Injera, a fermented thin flatbread made of a native grain, teff, is a staple food for people in what landlocked African country?	Ethiopia
Eating pre-dinner finger foods or appetizers, known locally as tapas, is a common practice among the natives of Zaragoza, a city on the Ebro River. Tapas are considered to be a traditional part of the cuisine of what country?	Spain

Question	Answer
Idli, dosa, and vada are typical food items of Tamil- and Telugu-speaking people in the southern parts of which country?	India
Brought to the Caribbean from West Africa on slave ships, the ackee fruit along with saltfish is the national dish of what country?	Jamaica
Izakayas are establishments that serve food to accompany drinks. Customers in Izakayas typically sit on tatami mats and dine from low tables. Izakayas are popular after-work gathering places in what Asian country?	Japan
Pesto sauce is believed to have originated in what northwestern Italian coastal region whose biggest city, Genoa, is the birthplace of Christopher Columbus?	Liguria
Ambuyat, a dish made of sago, is often eaten using chandas, a two pronged bamboo stick similar in ways to both chopsticks and forks. Ambuyat is part of the national cuisine of what small predominantly Muslim Asian country?	Brunei

Question	Answer
Chapter 17. Cultural Geography: Language	
French-speaking people of Canada are concentrated mostly in which province?	Quebec
What is the official language of Liechtenstein and its neighbor, Austria?	German
Which Canadian city has the most French-speaking people?	Montreal
The Yiddish language is associated with people practicing what religion—Judaism, Buddhism, or Islam?	Judaism
Dutch is the mostly widely spoken language in what small South American country?	Suriname
Bollywood, the Mumbai-based film industry, produces films mostly in what language that is spoken by about 41 percent of the people in India?	Hindi
Firdausi, one of the classical and most famous poets from ancient Iran, wrote mostly in what language?	Persian
The holy books of Hinduism are originally written in what ancient language?	Sanskrit
Afrikaans, English, Tswana, and Xhosa are among the 11 official languages in which country?	South Africa
Belgium's largest linguistic group, the Flemings, is concentrated in the region called Flanders. What is the native language of the Flemings?	Dutch
What language, spoken in East Asia, is traditionally written in three forms, Kanji, Hiragana, and Katakana, although romanization is also used?	Japanese
What is the official and most widely used language in Bangladesh?	Bengali or Bangla
The city of Quetta, where you can hear people speaking Urdu, Balochi, and Pashto, is in which country?	Pakistan
What is the major spoken language of the Democratic Republic of the Congo, a former Belgian colony that received independence in 1960?	French
Malagasy is one of the two official languages of what island country that was once a French colony?	Madagascar
Dutch is a not widely spoken in which country—the Netherlands, Suriname, or Equatorial Guinea?	Equatorial Guinea
What is the most widely spoken language of the Walloons in Belgium?	French
Name the landlocked European nation whose official language is German, which has no army, and which adopted the Swiss franc as its currency in 1921.	Liechtenstein

Question	Answer
French, Romansh, Italian, and what other language are the most widely spoken languages in Switzerland?	German
Although Urdu is the national language, about 44 percent of its people claim Punjabi as their native language in which country?	Pakistan
What is the official language in Mozambique and Angola?	Portuguese
What African language is a lingua franca in much of East Africa and the Democratic Republic of the Congo and is a national or official language of Tanzania and Kenya?	Swahili
Which of the 11 official languages of South Africa is claimed as the mother tongue by most people in that country—Zulu, Afrikaans, or English?	Zulu
What is the most widely spoken language in the South American capital city of Paramaribo?	Dutch
The language spoken in the Balearic Islands and the city of Barcelona is also the official language of Andorra. Name that language.	Catalan
What is the official language of Brunei?	Malay
Hindi is not the most widely spoken language in which Indian state—Bihar, Uttar Pradesh, or Gujarat?	Gujarat
The Saami language, classified as an Uralic language, is spoken by the Saami people in what part of the Europe—northern Spain, northern Scandinavia, or southern Balkan Peninsula?	Northern Scandinavia
What language, spoken by about 10 million indigenous people today, was the official language of the Inca Empire?	Quechua or Quichua
Dzongkha is widely spoken in what landlocked Himalayan kingdom?	Bhutan

Question	Answer
Chapter 18. Cultural Geography: Religion	
Which major religion has the most followers in the world?	Christianity
The majority of the followers of the Church of Jesus Christ of Latter-day Saints, or the Mormon Church, live in what U.S. state?	Utah
During the holy month of Ramadan, people practicing what religion fast until sunset?	Islam
What major world religion with about 12 million followers was established in the U.S. in 1830 by Joseph Smith?	Church of Jesus Christ of Latter-day Saints or Mormon Church
Which country does not have a majority Christian population—Turkey, the Philippines, or Armenia?	Turkey
Which country has the most followers of Islam?	Indonesia
Visitors must remove their shoes before entering the Shwedagon Pagoda, also known as the golden pagoda, which overlooks the city of Yangon in what Buddhist country?	Myanmar
Brahma, Vishnu, and Shiva are the three main deities of what religion practiced in Nepal?	Hinduism
What major religion was founded in northeastern India based on the teachings of Siddhartha Gautama?	Buddhism
Which continent has the most Roman Catholic people?	South America
According to the Old Testament, Noah's ark landed on the Mount Ararat after the deluge. Mount Ararat, a peak perpetually covered with snow, is located in which present-day country near its border with Armenia and Iran?	Turkey
Although people who practice this religion constitute only 12 percent of India's population, only two other countries have more people of this religion than India. Name this religion.	Islam
What religion that has about one billion followers celebrates Diwali, a festival of lights?	Hinduism
What major religion that started in India in about 550 BC, travelled eastward, and now has a lot more followers outside India than in India.	Buddhism
The Rohingya people, a Muslim ethnic group of Rakhine state in Myanmar, have fled to what predominantly Muslim neighboring country to avoid persecution?	Bangladesh
What is the only major Indonesian island with a Hindu majority?	Bali

Question	Answer
The Golden Temple in the city of Amritsar, Punjab, India, is one of the holiest places for people practicing what religion?	Sikhism
What major religion has two branches known as Theravada and Mahayana?	Buddhism
Mecca and what other city in Saudi Arabia are considered to be holiest places for Muslims?	Medina
Although Buddhism is the most widely practiced religion in Sri Lanka, about 15 percent of the population practice what other religion?	Hinduism
Biswa Ijtema, which means world congregation in the Bengali language, is an annual gathering of millions of Muslim devotees that takes place near the city of Tongi on the Turag River. Biswa Ijtema takes place in what country?	Bangladesh
What is the most widely practiced religion in Albania and Kosovo?	Islam
Ireland and which other small European island country are majority Roman Catholic?	Malta
A gurudwara is a place of worship for people practicing what religion?	Sikhism
Located about 11 miles east of Yogyakarta City, Prambanan, built in the ninth century, is the largest Hindu temple in which country?	Indonesia
The town of Shravana Belagola, in the state of Karnataka, is one of the most important pilgrim centers for followers of the Jain religion. In which country is Shravana Belagola?	India
Afaq Khoja was an important Sufi religious leader in the 17th century. To which present-day country would you go to see Afaq Khoja's tomb near the city of Kashgar in the Tarim Basin?	China
Mt. Gunung Agung, the highest peak on the island of Bali in Indonesia, is an important site to adherents of what religion?	Hinduism

Question	Answer
Chapter 19. Cultural Geography: Arts and Traditional Clothing	
The bagpipe, a wind instrument consisting of a leather bag with pipes with finger holes, is most commonly associated with the Celtic people of what island country?	the U.K.
Baggy trousers called bombachas and wide-brimmed felt hats are traditional dress for gauchos from what continent?	South America
Mariachi bands playing traditional music wear the charro suit consisting of a heavily embroidered jacket and matching pants and a wide brimmed hat known as a sombrero. Which country would you visit to listen to mariachi bands in the states of Zacatecas, Michoacán, and Nayarit?	Mexico
Unmarried women and young girls in Pakistan and what other country to its east wear long flowing trousers called shalwar and a long blouse called a kameez?	India
The kilt, a knee-length, skirt-like garment that is pleated at the back but has a plain front, is associated with what people?	Scots
The jarjar, a frame drum traditional to the folk music of the indigenous people of the Kamchatka Peninsula, is used in what country?	Russia
The nyatiti is a type of stringed folk instrument native to the western part of what East African country whose largest seaport city is Mombasa?	Kenya
The sarong, a traditional garment consisting of a length of fabric wrapped and tied around the body at the waist or under the arms, is worn by men and women in several countries on what continent?	Asia
Ikebana, an ancient art of arranging flowers that has been in practice for more than 600 years is associated with what Asian island country?	Japan
The nyckelharpa is a type of keyed fiddle that can be heard on the western banks of the Gulf of Bothnia in what country?	Sweden
On special occasions such as weddings and funerals, women from what island country wear a traditional robe called a kimono that is tied around the waist with a sash called an obi and worn with sandals called zori?	Japan
Traditionally associated with the Shona people, the mbira, a thumb piano made of forged iron keys bound to a wooden box, is the most important instrument in the music and culture of what African country that was formerly known as Southern Rhodesia?	Zimbabwe
The khaen, a mouth organ made of a reed and bamboo pipes, is traditional in the music of what landlocked Indo-Chinese country?	Laos
The huipil is a loose, richly embroidered traditional garment worn by indigenous Maya women in which part of the world—Central America, West Asia, or southern Africa?	Central America

Question	Answer
Women from which Asian country with more than a billion people wear the sari, a colorful garment consisting of a single six-meter-long piece of cloth draped around the body as a long dress?	India
The dombra, a two-stringed lute usually played in a galloping rhythm, is a folk instrument of which Central Asian country touching both the Caspian and Aral Seas?	Kazakhstan
Klompen, shoes made entirely of wood, are commonly associated with rural areas of which European country?	the Netherlands
The gho is a knee-length robe tied at the waist and the kira is an ankle-length dress consisting of a rectangular piece of fabric wrapped around the body and pinned at shoulders. The gho and kira are traditional dresses for men and women in the cities of Thimpu and Phuntsholing. To which small landlocked country would you go to see men and women wearing the gho and kira?	Bhutan
Men and women in the cities of Fez and Marrakech wear long, full sleeved, loosely fitted, hooded robes called djellaba. The djellaba is traditional dress in what African country?	Morocco
Lederhosen, leather shorts for men and boys and often worn with suspenders, are traditionally associated with what country?	Germany
Flying kites is a popular activity during springtime in the cities of Lahore and Rawalpindi in which country?	Pakistan
Andalusia, a region where flamenco dance is considered to have originated, is part of which country?	Spain
The hanbok, known as the choson-ot in the northern parts of the peninsula, is a dress characterized by vibrant colors and simple lines. The hanbok is the traditional dress of people on what Asian peninsula?	Korean
Songs for bhangra, a colorful vibrant dance, are written in what language spoken by people in both India and Pakistan?	Punjabi
An icon of African cultural heritage around the world, kente cloth made by the Ashanti people is identified by its dazzling, multicolored patterns of bright colors, geometric shapes, and bold designs. Kente cloth is native to which West African country?	Ghana
Students interested in learning to create kakemono, a traditional art form of silk or paper wall hangings with painting or calligraphy, can travel to the city of Sendai in which country?	Japan
The dhoti is a traditional garment for men for the lower part of the body. It consists of a piece of unstitched cloth draped over the hips and legs. What country would you visit to see men wearing dhotis in the cities of Allahabad and Patna?	India

Question	Answer
The komuz, a small lute-like instrument with a long neck and three strings, is a traditional folk instrument of which country whose capital, in the Chu River Valley, was known as Frunze from 1926–1991?	Kyrgyzstan

Question	Answer
Chapter 20. Cultural Geography: Sports	
What southwestern U.S. city on the Salt River hosted Tostitos Fiesta Bowl game in 2014—Phoenix, Seattle, or Atlanta?	Phoenix
The Orange Bowl football game takes place annually in what U.S. state that leads the country in orange production—California, Florida, or Kansas?	Florida
Candlestick Park, Fisherman's Wharf, and Golden Gate Bridge are located in which city?	San Francisco
Wimbledon, one of the most prestigious tennis tournaments, is played in the suburbs of what European capital city?	London
The Preakness Stakes, a thoroughbred horse race, is held in May each year at Pimlico Race Course in the city of Baltimore. To which U.S. state would you go to see the Preakness Stakes?	Maryland
Nagano, the host city for the 1998 Winter Olympics, is located on the island of Honshu in which country?	Japan
The Belmont Stakes, a thoroughbred horse race and the final leg of the U.S. Triple Crown, is held in June at Belmont Park in the town of Hempstead in Nassau County on Long Island. What Atlantic coast state would you visit to see the Belmont Stakes?	New York
Bandy, a sport described as ice hockey with a ball, was played as a demonstration event when the Winter Olympics were held in Norway's largest city in 1952. Name this city.	Oslo
Roland Garros Stadium, where one of the Grand Slam tennis tournaments is played, is located in what European city?	Paris
The city of Pyeongchang, located about 45 miles south of the 38th parallel, will host the 2018 Winter Olympics. In which peninsular country is Pyeongchang located?	South Korea
The 2008 World Chess Championship between Viswanathan Anand and Vladimir Kramnik took place in what German city on the Rhine River that served as the capital of West Germany?	Bonn
Which team sport is considered to be of Native American origin—lacrosse, basketball, or ice hockey?	Lacrosse
Three Rivers Stadium, constructed in 1970 and demolished in 2001, near where Allegany and Monongahela Rivers join to form the Ohio River, was located in what city?	Pittsburgh
Hurling, a sport popular in the counties of Kilkenny and Tipperary, is considered native to which Gaelic country?	Ireland

Question	Answer
Buzkashi or kokpar is a sport in which teams on horseback compete to gain possession and propel an object to a scoring area. Buzkashi is a popular sport in what part of the world—Central Asia or Central America?	Central Asia
The Masters, one of the four major championships in professional golf, is held annually at the Augusta National Golf Club. Which U.S. state hosts the Masters?	Georgia
To watch a game of rugby in the city of Perth, which country would you visit?	Australia
Vuvuzela-wielding spectators were a common sight during the 2010 FIFA World Cup (soccer) held in what country?	South Africa
The Royal and Ancient Golf Club of St. Andrews, considered one of the oldest and most prestigious golf clubs in the world, is located in what European country?	the U.K. [Scotland]
South Korea and which other country co-hosted the soccer world cup in 2002?	Japan
The Chicago White Sox, Colorado Rockies, and Arizona Diamondbacks are some of the Major League Baseball teams that have done spring training in what Arizona city located about 100 miles south of Phoenix?	Tucson
The Indomitable Lions is the nick name for which African country's soccer team whose home stadium is in the city of Yaoundé?	Cameroon
The city of Turin, which hosted the Winter Olympics in 2006, is on the Po River in the northern part of which country?	Italy
Which city, the largest in the Canadian Province of British Columbia, hosted the 2010 Winter Olympics?	Vancouver
Galle International Stadium, where the game of cricket is played, has been rebuilt after a devastating tsunami hit the city of Galle on December 26, 2004. To which island country would you go to watch a game of cricket at Galle International Stadium?	Sri Lanka
What Caribbean country located in the Greater Antilles group of islands hosted the Commonwealth Games in 1966?	Jamaica
The Kentucky Derby, a famous horse race attended by more than 150,000 spectators, is held on the first Saturday of May at Churchill Downs racetrack in what city?	Louisville
Which African country hosted the All-Africa Games twice, in two different cities— once in its current capital city and once in a former capital city?	Nigeria
The city of Sochi, with the snowcapped Caucasus Mountains on the horizon, hosted the Winter Olympics in 2014. In which country is Sochi?	Russia

Question	Answer
The 2010 World Chess Championship between Viswanathan Anand and Veselin Topalov took place in what capital city whose landscape is defined by Mount Vitosha?	Sofia
What Atlantic port city, located about 230 miles southeast of Buenos Aires, hosted the 1995 Pan-American Games?	Mar del Plata

Question	Answer
Chapter 21. Economic Geography: Bridges, Causeways, and Tunnels	
The driving distance between the cities of Ningbo and Shanghai was reduced by 75 miles when the 22.5-mile-long Hangzhou Bay Bridge opened on May 2, 2008. In which country is Hangzhou Bay Bridge located?	China
The Channel Tunnel, known as the Chunnel, is a 31-mile-long undersea rail tunnel that connects which two countries?	the U.K. and France
The Mackinac Bridge, a suspension bridge spanning the Straits of Mackinac, connects the upper and lower peninsulas of what state in the U.S.?	Michigan
With around 150,000 vehicle crossings a day, the Fredhälls Tunnel in the city of Stockholm is one of the most traveled tunnels in Europe. In which country is Fredhälls Tunnel located?	Sweden
The Strait of Messina Bridge upon its completion will provide a road connection to what large island from mainland Italy?	Sicily
To cross the Bosporus Strait by road you can take either the Boğaziçi Bridge or the Fatih Sultan Mehmet Bridge in what country?	Turkey
The George Washington Bridge, a double-decked suspension bridge with 14 lanes of travel, carried about 102 million vehicles in 2013 making it the world's busiest motor vehicle bridge. The George Washington Bridge connects which two U.S. states?	New Jersey and New York
The 10.7-mile-long Vasco da Gama Bridge spans what important river in Portugal?	Tagus River
Lincoln Tunnel and Holland Tunnel, which provide a road link between New Jersey and the borough of Manhattan, are under what body of water?	Hudson River
The Forth Road Bridge, which spans the Firth of Forth, connects the city of Edinburgh at South Queensferry to Fife at North Queensferry in which nation?	Scotland
The Lake Pontchartrain Causeway, which consists of two parallel bridges crossing Lake Pontchartrain, is about 24 miles long, making it the longest overwater bridge. The Lake Pontchartrain Causeway is in the southern part of which U.S. state?	Louisiana
An archipelago of about 35 specks and one large island, this country prospers by processing crude oil rather than drilling for it. Name this country in the Persian Gulf that is connected to Saudi Arabia by the 14.5-mile-long King Fahd Causeway.	Bahrain
The President Costa e Silva Bridge, locally known as The Rio-Niteroi Bridge, is a reinforced concrete structure that connects the cities of Niteroi and the second largest city in Brazil. Name this city in Brazil.	Rio de Janeiro
The San Mateo-Hayward Bridge near the city of Oakland in California spans what bay?	San Francisco Bay

Question	Answer
N'Djamena, the capital of Chad, is connected by a bridge across the Chari River to the town of Kousséri in what neighboring country?	Cameroon
The Seikan Tunnel is a 33.5-mile-long railway tunnel going under the Tsugaru Strait and connecting Japan's Honshu Island with what island to its north?	Hokkaido
The Verrazano-Narrows Bridge, which connects the boroughs of Staten Island and Brooklyn, is the starting point of what famous running race?	New York City Marathon
The San Juanico Bridge spans the San Juanico Strait and connects the islands of Leyte and Samar. The San Juanico Bridge is the longest bridge spanning a body of sea water in what Asian country?	the Philippines
The Chesapeake Bay Bridge–Tunnel, a 23-mile-long facility that crosses the mouth of the Chesapeake Bay, is in which U.S. state?	Virginia
The eight-mile-long confederation bridge spanning the Northumberland Strait links Price Edward Island with what Canadian province?	New Brunswick
The Titlis Cliff Walk is a pedestrian suspension bridge that is 320 feet long and only 3 feet wide and opened in December, 2012. At 10,000 feet above sea level, the Titlis Cliff Walk is Europe's highest suspension bridge. To which landlocked country would you go to walk on this bridge overlooking Alpine glaciers?	Switzerland
The Akashi-Kaikyo Bridge that spans the Akashi Strait in Japan is about 2.5 miles long and is considered to be the world's longest suspension bridge. It links Awaji Island to the city of Kobe on what island?	Honshu
The 4.8-mile-long Oresund Bridge and the 2.5-mile-long Drogden Tunnel connect what two countries?	Denmark and Sweden
The Donghai Bridge is a 20-mile-long cross-sea bridge that connects the city of Shanghai and the offshore deepwater port of Yangshan. The Donghai Bridge spans what body of water?	Hangzhou Bay (or East China Sea)
The Bridge of the Americas and the Centennial Bridge span what important shipping canal?	Panama Canal
Designed by French Architect Gustave Eiffel of Eiffel Tower fame, the Long Bien Bridge was completed in 1902. This cantilever bridge provides stunning views across the Red River. Today, the Long Bien Bridge is a beloved historic landmark of what Vietnamese city?	Hanoi
The Great Belt Fixed Link, which consists of bridges and tunnels that connect the islands of Zealand and Funen, is in which country?	Denmark
The Mubarak Peace Bridge, El Ferdan Railway Bridge, and Ahmed Hamdi Tunnel cross what important shipping lane?	Suez Canal

Question	Answer
What strait would a proposed bridge connecting the Indonesian islands of Java and Sumatra span?	Sunda Strait
The Bang Na Expressway is a 34-mile-long elevated highway constructed to alleviate traffic problems in what Asian capital city at the mouth of the Chao Phraya River?	Bangkok
In June 2013, the New Europe Bridge opened connecting the cities of Calafat in Romania to Vidin in Bulgaria. The New Europe Bridge spans what important river?	Danube River
The Glienicke Bridge, popularly known as the "Bridge of Spies" during the Cold War, spans the Havel River. The Glienicke Bridge connects the city of Potsdam to what capital city?	Berlin

Question	Answer
Chapter 22. Economic Geography: Transportation	
The 27-mile-long Welland Canal was dug in Canada between Lake Erie and Lake Ontario so ships can bypass what waterfalls?	Niagara Falls
Qantas Airways, nicknamed "The Flying Kangaroo," is the national airline of which country?	Australia
O'Hare International Airport, which is about 15 miles west of Lake Michigan, is in which city?	Chicago
Which canal is older—the Suez or Panama Canal?	Suez Canal
Name the highly urbanized island country located at the southern tip of the Malay Peninsula that has one of the world's busiest ports.	Singapore
Officially opened on September 28, 2006, to replace the aging Don Muang Airport, Bangkok's Suvarnabhumi Airport is the largest airport in which Asian country?	Thailand
Although used mainly by tourists these days, gondolas have been the most common method of transportation for centuries in what Italian city on the Adriatic Sea?	Venice
A major gateway for U.S.–Asian trade, Long Beach is one of the busiest seaports in which U.S. state?	California
Chhatrapati Shivaji International Airport and Indira Gandhi International Airport are located in which country?	India
The Trans-Siberian Railway, which extends over 5,500 miles east to west, is located in what country?	Russia
All Nippon Airways, whose main international hubs are at Narita International Airport and Kansai International Airport, is which country's second largest international airline?	Japan
On July 6, 2013, a train hauling two million gallons of crude oil derailed and exploded in the Canadian town of Lac-Mégantic, killing 47 people. The town of Lac-Mégantic, located about 22 miles west of Maine border, is in which Canadian province?	Quebec
Rotterdam, Europe's busiest port, is situated in the Rhine River Delta in which country?	the Netherlands
Serving as a hub for Delta Airlines, Hartsfield-Jackson International Airport is the world's busiest airport in terms of passenger traffic. In which southern city in the U.S. is Hartsfield International Airport located?	Atlanta
Lufthansa, whose corporate headquarters is located in the city of Cologne, is the national airlines of which country?	Germany

Question	Answer
The historic Erie Canal, dug in early 1800s, provided the first transportation route between the eastern seaboard at New York City and the western interior along the Great Lakes. The Erie Canal connects Lake Erie to what river?	Hudson River
El Al, whose hub is located at Ben Gurion International Airport, is the national airline for which Middle Eastern country?	Israel
Heathrow Airport handles more international passenger traffic than any other airport in the world. In which European city is Heathrow Airport located?	London
Because it serves as a hub for Federal Express shipments, the airport in what city by the Mississippi River in Tennessee handles the most cargo traffic by volume annually?	Memphis
Incheon International Airport, which is one of Asia's largest and busiest airports, is located in which peninsular country?	South Korea
The Volga-Don Shipping Canal, a 63-mile-long canal together with the lower Volga and the lower Don Rivers, provides the most direct navigable connection between the Sea of Azov and what other body of water?	Caspian Sea
The 61-mile-long Kiel Canal in Germany provides a shorter route for ships between what two large bodies of water?	North Sea and Baltic Sea
Germany's busiest airport in terms of passenger traffic is located in which city?	Frankfurt
The Corinth Canal dug across the Isthmus of Corinth in late 1800s to connect the Gulf of Corinth with the Saronic Gulf in the Aegean Sea is in what country?	Greece
Charles de Gaulle Airport is located in which European city that is one of the world's leading business, cultural, and fashion centers?	Paris
Ships can navigate 900 miles upstream on the Amazon River to what port city at the confluence of the Rio Negro and the Amazon River?	Manaus
Chiba, one the world's busiest seaports, is located about 25 miles south west of Narita International Airport. Chiba is in which country?	Japan
The Buffalo Bayou, a waterway that was developed into a busy shipping channel, connects what major Texas interior port city to the Gulf of Mexico?	Houston
Ships traveling what important waterway go through Gatun, Pedro Miguel, and Miraflores Locks?	Panama Canal
Where is the headquarters of Cathay Pacific Airways located?	Hong Kong
The Belomorkanal, a ship canal that joins the White Sea and the Baltic Sea, is in which country?	Russia

Question	Answer
Aer Lingus and Ryanair are the two biggest airlines in which European country?	Ireland
Atlas Blue is a low-cost airline based in the city of Marrakech in which country?	Morocco
The Great Bitter Lake is part of what international waterway that opened in 1869?	Suez Canal

Question	Answer
Chapter 23. Economic Geography: Other Aspects	
The rial is the official currency of what oil-producing country—Iran or Singapore?	Iran
Subsistence agriculture is generally observed in what countries—less developed countries, developed countries, or capitalistic countries?	LDCs
The most populated country in Africa is also Africa's leading crude oil producer. Name this country.	Nigeria
Which country is world's biggest consumer of energy?	U.S.A.
The CFA franc is the official monetary unit of more than 10 countries in the northern parts of what continent?	Africa
Offshore oil drilling in the Gulf of Guinea is an important economic activity in what continent—Africa or Europe?	Africa
Viticulture is the study and cultivation of grapes and grape vines. Viticulture is an important economic activity in which California valley—Napa Valley or Silicon Valley?	Napa Valley
In which country is the krona the official currency—Sweden or Germany?	Sweden
Oxford and Cambridge Universities, the two oldest surviving universities in the English-speaking world, are in what country?	the U.K.
The U.A.E. uses the process of desalination for producing what natural substance?	Fresh water
Which country is not a major producer of nutmeg—Grenada, Barbados, or Indonesia?	Barbados
The baht is the currency of what Southeast Asian country—Thailand or Singapore?	Thailand
Which European country is famous for cut flowers and Edam and Gouda cheeses?	the Netherlands
What is the official currency of Ecuador and El Salvador?	U.S. dollar
Charles Darwin is pictured on the 10 pound sterling bill of what country?	the U.K.
The sturgeon fish of the Caspian Sea, which can live to over 100 years but mature slowly, are being fished out of existence for their roe or eggs to make what luxury food item?	Caviar
Brazil and what other South American country are among the world's leading producers of coffee?	Colombia
What industry contributes more than 60 percent of Iceland's export revenue?	Fishing

Question	Answer
China and what other neighboring country are the world's top two producers of tea?	India
The kina replaced the Australian dollar as the official currency of what island country bordering Indonesia?	Papua New Guinea
In the last two decades, what renewable energy source has been harnessed with greater success in open treeless areas and mountain passes?	Wind
True or False—the euro is the official currency of French Guiana?	True
What Scandinavian country's economy improved tremendously with the discovery of oil and gas in adjacent waters in the late 1960s?	Norway
Indonesia and Vietnam are leading Asian producers of what beverage crop?	Coffee
The term conurbation refers to an area formed when two or more of what entities grow and eventually merge together?	Cities
Aegean Airlines is one of the chief airlines of what country that is a member of the European Union?	Greece
The city of Antwerp, famous for its diamond trade, is in what low country?	Belgium
Centered around the cities of Midland and Odessa, the Permian Basin is a home to a large oil and natural gas producing region. The Permian Basin is mostly in what U.S. state?	Texas
What Baltic country adopted the euro as its official currency on January 1, 2014?	Latvia
What is the term for the government system led by one or more religious leaders?	Theocracy
The won is to South Korea as the pula is to what?	Botswana
Although the ngultrum is the official currency, the Indian rupee is legal tender in what landlocked mountainous country?	Bhutan
What industry/activity constitutes nearly half of Brunei's gross domestic product?	Crude oil and natural gas production
Introduced by the British during colonial times, tea has become a major source of export revenue for what East African country?	Kenya
Tea exports are a major source of export revenue for what island country?	Sri Lanka
Which two West African countries produce more than half of the world's cocoa beans?	Cote d'Ivoire and Ghana

Question	Answer
A Lorenz curve or a Gini coefficient may be used for measuring what aspect of a country's development—income inequality, trade surplus, or labor productivity?	Income inequality
Which country does not have a trade surplus—U.S.A., China, or Germany?	U.S.A.
What term is used to describe a community, generally an urban district, with little or no access to supermarkets for buying healthier food items but often served by plenty of fast food restaurants?	Food Desert
Which country is not a major exporter of rice—U.S.A., Thailand, or Japan?	Japan
The production of oil from the Mangala oil field in the Barmer Basin in the state of Rajasthan is supposed to significantly cut what Asian country's energy imports?	India
Which country does not use the euro as its currency—Ireland, the U.K., or Finland?	the U.K.
The Yamal Peninsula, home to the Nenets people, possesses one of the world's largest natural gas reserves. The Yamal Peninsula is in which country?	Russia
The currency of what former Portuguese colony in Africa is the metical?	Mozambique
Rare earths are a group of 17 elements that are crucial for manufacturing many high tech products. With over 95 percent of world's production, which Asian country has a monopoly on the rare earths trade?	China
What small landlocked African monarchy's unit of currency is the lilangeni?	Swaziland

Question	Answer
Chapter 24. Find the Odd Item Out: United States	
Which state does not border Mexico—Arizona, New Mexico, or Nevada?	Nevada
Which tourist attraction is not in New York state—Ellis Island, Time Square, or Plymouth Rock?	Plymouth Rock
Which present-day state is not on the historic Oregon Trail—Nebraska, North Dakota, or Idaho?	North Dakota
Which landmark is not in Texas—the Gateway Arch, the Alamo, or the San Jacinto Monument?	Gateway Arch
Which state does not border any other state—Vermont, Alaska, or Maine?	Alaska
Which state did not secede from the Union during the Civil War—South Carolina, Pennsylvania, or Alabama?	Pennsylvania
Which state does not border Washington D.C.—Maryland, Virginia, or Pennsylvania?	Pennsylvania
Which state is not in the Plains—South Dakota, Kansas, or Utah?	Utah
Which state does not have a national park—Arizona, Utah, or Iowa?	Iowa
Which state does not have a mountain peak above 12,000 feet—California, Colorado, or Delaware?	Delaware
Which state is not considered to be a part of New England—Connecticut, Vermont, or Delaware?	Delaware
Which city does not have Atlantic seacoast—Boston, Atlanta, or Miami?	Atlanta
Which state does not meet at the four corners—Utah, Colorado, or Wyoming?	Wyoming
Which state is not south of the Mason-Dixon line—Virginia, North Carolina, or Pennsylvania?	Pennsylvania
Which city is not in Tornado Alley—Tulsa, Reno, or Topeka?	Reno
Which state does not have a coastline—New Hampshire, Vermont, or Delaware?	Vermont
Which state did not secede to join the Confederacy during the Civil War—Georgia, North Carolina, or Maryland?	Maryland
Which state does not have a coastline on Chesapeake Bay—Maryland, Virginia, or Delaware?	Delaware

Question	Answer
Which state does not have a port city on the Gulf of Mexico—Alabama, Louisiana, or Georgia?	Georgia
Which state is not entirely south of Kentucky—Tennessee, Iowa, or Georgia?	Iowa
Which is not a tributary of the Mississippi River—the Arkansas River, Red River, or Susquehanna River?	Susquehanna River
Tourism is not a major industry in which city—Las Vegas, Des Moines, or Orlando?	Des Moines
Which state is not a major producer of corn—Illinois, Iowa, or Nevada?	Nevada
Which is not a port city in California—Long Beach, San Diego, or Sacramento?	Sacramento
Which state does not touch Tennessee—Arkansas, Missouri, or South Carolina?	South Carolina
Which city is not on the Ohio River—Cincinnati, Lexington, or Louisville?	Lexington
Which city is not in Texas—Lubbock, Amarillo, or Shreveport?	Shreveport
The Missouri River does not flow through which state—North Dakota, Oregon, or Montana?	Oregon
Which national park is not east of the Mississippi River—Olympic NP, Dry Tortugas NP, or Acadia NP?	Olympic NP
Which state is not a producer of crude oil—Alaska, Texas, or Arizona?	Arizona
Which state is not a major producer of cotton—Texas, Mississippi, or Florida?	Florida
Which city is not at the same latitude as the other two—Las Vegas, Tulsa, or Omaha?	Omaha
Which U.S. city is not on the Mexican border—El Paso in Texas, Laredo in Texas, or Phoenix in Arizona?	Phoenix
Which U.S. city does not have a majority of its population that is of Hispanic origin—San Antonio, Miami, or Atlanta?	Atlanta
At least 20 percent of its population is not African American in which state—Mississippi, Georgia, or Texas?	Texas
Which island is not a part of Texas—Mustang Island, Matagorda Island, or Santa Catalina Island?	Santa Catalina Island
Which river does not have headwaters in the state of Colorado—the Arkansas River, South Platte River, or Snake River?	Snake River

Question	Answer
Which state cannot be reached by a boat from the St. Lawrence waterway—Ohio, Minnesota, or West Virginia?	West Virginia
Which city is not on the Missouri River—Kansas City, Omaha, or Fargo?	Fargo
Asian Americans do not constitute at least 10 percent of which state's population—Illinois, California, or Hawaii?	Illinois
Which river does not empty into the Gulf of Mexico—the Savannah River, Mississippi River, or Brazos River?	Savannah River
Which national park is not in Utah—Grand Teton NP, Canyonlands NP, or Bryce Canyon NP?	Grand Teton NP
Which river is not directly connected to Lake St. Clair—the St. Clair River, Detroit River, or Flint River?	Flint River
Which Mexican city is not on the U.S. border—Hermosillo, Mexicali, or Nogales?	Hermosillo
Which city is not at the same longitude as the other two—Knoxville in Tennessee, Mobile in Alabama, or Milwaukee in Wisconsin?	Knoxville
People of Hispanic origin do not constitute at least 10 percent of which state's population—Colorado, Nevada, or Montana?	Montana
Which river does not empty into Chesapeake bay—the Susquehanna River, Potomac River, or Delaware River?	Delaware River
Which Mexican state does not touch the U.S.—Durango, Chihuahua, or Coahuila?	Durango
Which mountain range is not in Alaska—the Chugach Mountains, Brooks Range, or Lewis Range?	Lewis Range
Which state is not a major producer of rice—Arkansas, Iowa, or California?	Iowa

Question	Answer
Chapter 25. Find the Odd Item Out: World	
Which is not a territory in Canada—Yukon, Nunavut, or Galapagos?	Galapagos
Which desert is not in Africa—the Gobi, Kalahari, or Sahara?	Gobi
Which capital city is not in South America—Asunción, Santiago, or Santa Domingo?	Santa Domingo
Which waterfall is not in the Western Hemisphere—Angel, Tugela, or Iguacu?	Tugela
Which people are not native to the Southern Hemisphere—Maori, Aborigines, or Ainu?	Ainu
Which strait is not in the Southern Hemisphere—the Torres Strait, Bass Strait, or Bering Strait?	Bering Strait
Which river is not in Asia—the Narmada, Irrawaddy, or Tagus?	Tagus River
Which river does not flow through India—the Ganges, Orinoco, or Godavari?	Orinoco
Which is not a city in New Zealand—Christchurch, Auckland, or Adelaide?	Adelaide
Which is not a mountain range in Europe—the Taurus, Apennine, or Carpathian Mountains?	Taurus
Which strait is not crossed when traveling from Ukraine to the U.K. by ship—the Bosporus Strait, Strait of Gibraltar, or Cook Strait?	Cook Strait
Which mountain range is not in Asia—the Jura, Zagros, or Kunlun Mountains?	Jura
Which is not an island country in the Pacific Ocean—Tuvalu, Togo, or Tonga?	Togo
Arabic is not an official language in which country—Iran, Algeria, or Lebanon?	Iran
Which is not an island in Indonesia—Sulawesi, Sumatra, or Socotra?	Socotra
Which is not a mountain range in Africa—the Drakensberg, Atlas, or Taurus Mountains?	Taurus
Which country does not have a coast on the Caspian Sea—Iran, Azerbaijan, or Uzbekistan?	Uzbekistan
Which food it not a traditional Middle Eastern dish—hummus, falafel, or kimchi?	Kimchi
Which is not a mountain range in Iran—the Zagros, Elburz, or Pamir Mountains?	Pamirs
Which is not a seaport city—Shanghai, Karachi, or Tehran?	Tehran

Question	Answer
Which country was not a former colony of the U.K.—India, Thailand, or Sri Lanka?	Thailand
Islam is not the major religion in which country—Sri Lanka, Malaysia, or Turkey?	Sri Lanka
Which country does not have a coast on the Aral Sea—Uzbekistan, Kazakhstan, or Turkmenistan?	Turkmenistan
Which capital city is not on the Danube River—Bratislava, Budapest, or Bucharest?	Bucharest
Which river does not empty into the Gulf of Guinea—the Niger, Volta, or Gambia?	Gambia River
Which island is not divided between two or more countries—Tierra del Fuego, Mindanao, or Hispaniola?	Mindanao
Which is not a U.S. overseas territory—the Northern Mariana Islands, Guam, or the Cook Islands?	Cook Islands
Which is not a seaport city—Pusan, Kathmandu, or Kobe?	Kathmandu
Which river touches more than one country—the Yangtze, Ob, or Mekong?	Mekong River
Which musical instrument is not native to India—the sitar, veena, or sistrum?	Sistrum
Urdu is not an official language in which country—India, Turkey, or Pakistan?	Turkey
Which country does not have a shoreline on the Gulf of Finland—Russia, Estonia, or Lithuania?	Lithuania
Which country is not located on the Gulf of Guinea—Nigeria, Cameroon, or Mauritania?	Mauritania
Which strait is not travelled by an oil tanker taking oil directly from Kuwait to Japan—the Strait of Hormuz, Strait of Malacca, or Strait of Otranto?	Strait of Otranto
Brazil is not a major exporter of which commodity—coffee, soybeans, or rice?	Rice
Which country is not a member of the North Atlantic Treaty Organization (NATO)—Turkey, Greece, or Russia?	Russia
Which country does not border China—North Korea, Thailand, or Kyrgyzstan?	Thailand
Catholic Christians are not the majority in which country—France, Greece, or Argentina?	Greece
Which river does not empty into the Gulf of Mexico—the Rio Grande, Savannah, or Pearl?	Savannah

Question	Answer
Which country is not a member of the European Union—Latvia, Poland, or Ukraine?	Ukraine
The Philippines does not have a coast on which sea—the Sulu Sea, South China Sea, or Timor Sea?	Timor Sea
Which country does not use euros as its official currency—Norway, Germany, or Spain?	Norway
Which country is not a member of the Organization of the Petroleum Exporting Countries (OPEC)—Egypt, Saudi Arabia, or Venezuela?	Egypt
Which islands do not belong to India—the Maldives, the Andaman Islands, or Lakshadweep?	the Maldives
Which is not a major language in India—Bengali, Telugu, or Tagalog?	Tagalog
Which island is not part of the Windward Islands group in the Caribbean Sea—Saint Kitts, Saint Lucia, or Martinique?	Saint Kitts
Which river does not contribute water to the Ganges River—the Yamuna, Krishna, or Chambal?	Krishna
Which is not a British overseas territory—the Pitcairn Group of Islands, Ascension Island, or Johnston Atoll?	Johnston Atoll
Which Mexican state does not border Guatemala—Chiapas, Sinaloa, or Campeche?	Sinaloa

Question	Answer
Chapter 26. Sort Them Out: United States	
Arrange these states from north to south—Florida, Kentucky, and New Hampshire.	New Hampshire, Kentucky, Florida
Arrange these states by land area, from largest to smallest—Montana, Vermont, and Georgia.	Montana, Georgia, Vermont
Arrange these mountain ranges from west to east—the Appalachians, Sierra Nevadas, and Rockies.	Sierra Nevadas, Rockies, Appalachians
Arrange these cities from west to east—Detroit, Miami, and Phoenix.	Phoenix, Detroit, Miami
Arrange these rivers from west to east—the Savannah, Red, and Columbia Rivers.	Columbia, Red, Savannah Rivers
Arrange these states from most populated to least populated—Wyoming, Texas, and New Jersey.	Texas, New Jersey, Wyoming
Arrange these lakes from largest to smallest in surface area—Superior, Salt Lake, and Ontario.	Superior, Ontario, Salt Lake
Arrange these states by the length of shorelines on the Great Lakes, from the longest to the shortest—Michigan, Minnesota, and Pennsylvania.	Michigan, Minnesota, Pennsylvania
Arrange these mountain peaks by height, from the highest to the lowest—Mount Denali, Mount Elbert, and Mount Whitney.	Denali, Whitney, Elbert
Arrange these cities from upstream to downstream on the Mississippi River—Memphis, Vicksburg, and St. Louis.	St Louis, Memphis, Vicksburg
Arrange these states by the length of their Atlantic coastline, from the longest to the shortest—North Carolina, Maryland, and Virginia.	North Carolina, Virginia, Maryland
Arrange these states from most densely populated to least densely populated—Georgia, New Jersey, and Montana.	New Jersey, Georgia, Montana.
Arrange these cities from upstream to downstream on the Ohio River—Pittsburgh, Louisville, and Cincinnati.	Pittsburg, Cincinnati, Louisville,
Arrange these states from the oldest to the newest in terms of their date of admission to the U.S.A. as a state—Vermont, Arizona, and Utah.	Vermont, Utah, Arizona
Arrange these states by the length of their Canadian border, from the longest to the shortest—New Hampshire, Vermont, and Minnesota.	Minnesota, Vermont, New Hampshire
Arrange these states in terms of corn production from the highest to the lowest—Oklahoma, Missouri, and Illinois.	Illinois, Missouri, Oklahoma

Question	Answer
Arrange these cities from upstream to downstream on the Missouri River—Jefferson City, Bismarck, and Pierre.	Bismarck, Pierre, Jefferson City
Arrange these states by the length of their Mexican border, from the longest to the shortest—New Mexico, California, and Arizona.	Arizona, New Mexico, California
Arrange these mountain peaks from the highest to lowest—Mount Whitney, Mount Olympus, and Mount Logan.	Mt. Logan, Mt. Whitney, Mt. Olympus
Arrange these U.S. states by the number of other U.S. states they touch, from the most to the least—Idaho, South Carolina, and Missouri.	Missouri, Idaho, South Carolina
Arrange these states by total number of African Americans, from the highest to the lowest—New York, Arizona, and, Mississippi.	New York, Mississippi, Arizona
Arrange these rivers by length, from the longest to the shortest—the Yukon, Pecos, and Columbia Rivers.	Yukon, Columbia, Pecos
Arrange these states from most populated to least populated—Illinois, Florida, and Georgia.	Florida, Illinois, Georgia
Arrange these U.S. National Parks from west to east—Badlands NP, Congaree NP, and Haleakala NP.	Haleakala NP, Badlands NP, Congaree NP
Arrange these rivers by the number of states they touch, from the most to the least—the Hudson, Connecticut, and Snake Rivers.	Connecticut, Snake, Hudson Rivers

Question	Answer
Chapter 27. Sort Them Out: World	
Arrange these countries from most populous to least populous—India, U.S.A., and Germany.	India, U.S.A., Germany
Arrange these countries from the richest to the poorest based on the per capita income—China, Mali, and Kuwait.	Kuwait, China, Mali
Arrange these countries by the quantity of oil exported from the highest to the lowest—Saudi Arabia, Angola, and Venezuela.	Saudi Arabia, Venezuela, Angola
Arrange these islands from the biggest to the smallest by area—Crete, Baffin Island, and Tasmania.	Baffin Island, Tasmania, Crete
Arrange these mountain peaks from the tallest to the lowest—Uluru, Mont Blanc, and Kanchenjunga.	Kanchenjunga, Mont Blanc, Uluru
Arrange these countries by the number of people following Islam from the most to the least—Saudi Arabia, Indonesia, and India.	Indonesia, India, Saudi Arabia
Arrange these countries from north to south—Kenya, Denmark, and Comoros.	Denmark, Kenya, Comoros
Arrange these countries by the size of their GDP from the biggest to the smallest—Japan, Madagascar, and Brazil.	Japan, Brazil, Madagascar
Arrange these cities from upstream to downstream on the Danube River—Belgrade, Vienna, and Budapest.	Vienna, Budapest, Belgrade,
Arrange these countries by their energy consumption from the highest to the lowest—U.S.A., Italy, and India.	U.S.A., India, Italy
Arrange these continents by the number of countries in them, from the most to the least—Asia, Africa, and North America.	Africa, Asia, North America
Arrange these Caribbean island countries from west to east—Haiti, Jamaica, and Granada.	Jamaica, Haiti, Granada
Arrange these countries from most densely populated to least densely populated—Namibia, Singapore, and Guatemala.	Singapore, Guatemala, Namibia
Arrange these bodies of water in the order an oil tanker carrying oil from Kuwait to Japan will pass through—the South China Sea, the Strait of Malacca, and the Strait of Hormuz.	Strait of Hormuz, Strait of Malacca, South China Sea
Arrange these languages by the number of native speakers, from the most to the least—German, Bengali, and Spanish.	Spanish, Bengali, German
Arrange these cities from south to north—Hamburg, Rome, and Paris.	Rome, Paris, Hamburg

Be a Geo Bee

Question	Answer
Arrange these waterfalls by height, from the highest to the lowest—Vinnufossen, Hannoki, and Tugela.	Tugela, Vinnufossen, Hannoki
Arrange these European countries by the number of other countries they touch, from the most to the least—the Netherlands, Poland, and Italy.	Poland, Italy, the Netherlands.
Arrange these Canadian provinces by land area, from the biggest to the smallest—Quebec, Ontario, and Saskatchewan.	Quebec, Ontario, Saskatchewan
Arrange these islands from the most populated to the least populated—Honshu, Java, Great Britain.	Java, Honshu, Great Britain
Arrange these African countries by population, from the most populated to the least populated—Ethiopia, South Africa and Nigeria.	Nigeria, Ethiopia, South Africa
Arrange these bodies of water in the order you pass through as you go from Venice to Rome by a ship—Tyrrhenian Sea, Ionian Sea, and Adriatic Sea.	Adriatic Sea, Ionian Sea, Tyrrhenian Sea
Arrange these Mexican states by the length of their U.S. border, from longest to shortest—Chihuahua, Nuevo Leon, and Baja California.	Chihuahua, Baja California, Nuevo Leon
Arrange these African lakes by surface area, from the largest to the smallest—Lake Tanganyika, Lake Malawi, and Lake Victoria.	Victoria, Tanganyika, Malawi
Arrange these mountain peaks by height, from the highest to the lowest—Kilimanjaro, Elbrus, and Denali.	Denali, Kilimanjaro, Elbrus
Arrange these Asian rivers by the number of countries they touch, from the most to the least—the Mekong, Brahmaputra, and Amu Darya Rivers.	Mekong, Amu Darya, Brahmaputra Rivers

Question	Answer
Chapter 28. Famous Landmarks and Buildings	
The Gateway Arch, a 630-foot-tall stainless steel arch constructed to commemorate the westward expansion of the U.S., dominates the skyline of what city?	St. Louis
The Colón Theater in Buenos Aires is considered one of the world's finest opera houses. To which country would you go see a show in the Colón Theater?	Argentina
The Sydney Opera House on Bennelong Point in Sydney Harbor is one of the most recognizable buildings in the world. What country would you visit to see a show in the Sydney Opera House?	Australia
10 Downing Street in the city of Westminster is one of the most famous addresses in which country—the U.K. or Canada?	the U.K.
Plaza Mayor and Plaza Puerta del Sol are part of Madrid's historical center. To which country would you go to visit these two popular city squares?	Spain
The small and imposing statue of the Little Mermaid that sits on a rock in Copenhagen Harbor is an icon and a major tourist attraction in what country?	Denmark
In which city would you see Red Square and the ornate St. Basil's Cathedral with its onion-shaped domes?	Moscow
Uluru, also called Ayers Rock, is one the largest monoliths in the world and is a natural icon for what country?	Australia
Petronas Towers, the world's tallest twin towers, are located in what city?	Kuala Lumpur
The southeastern face of what mountain in South Dakota is the site of four gigantic carved sculptures depicting the faces of U.S. Presidents George Washington, Thomas Jefferson, Abraham Lincoln, and Theodore Roosevelt?	Mount Rushmore
In which South American city can tourists take a cable car ride to the top of Sugar Loaf Mountain, called Pão de Açúcar in Portuguese, and enjoy panoramic views of the famous Copacabana beach?	Rio de Janeiro
Located at the corner of 34th Street and 5th Avenue, what famous building completed in 1931 remained New York City's and the world's tallest building for over four decades?	Empire State Building
The small stretch of Lombard Street between Hyde and Leavenworth streets zigzags with eight sharp turns. Lombard Street, said to be one of the world's most crooked streets, is an attraction for drivers visiting what California city?	San Francisco
What famous building is located at 1600 Pennsylvania Avenue?	White House
La Plaza de la Constitución, the city hub and a public square that is often the site of major public ceremonies and military displays, is one of the main attractions of what large North American city?	Mexico City

Question	Answer
Cristo Redentor, a monumental statue of Christ on top of Corcovado Mountain, can be seen from all over what South American City?	Rio de Janeiro
Trafalgar Square is a popular tourist spot and is often the site of political demonstrations. Trafalgar Square is in the central part of what European capital city?	London
Our Lady of Peace of Yamoussoukro Basilica, considered to be the largest Christian church in the world, is in which African country?	Cote d'Ivoire
The Potala Palace, a treasure of Tibetan history, religion, and culture, is in which city?	Lhasa
What country would you visit to see the Sistine Chapel, which contains two of the world's most celebrated frescoes, *Genesis* and *The Last Judgment*?	Vatican City
Stonehenge, a prehistoric monument consisting of a circular group of large upright stones, is located in what plain in England?	Salisbury Plain
Built during the 12th century for King Suryavarman II, Angkor Wat is a renowned Hindu temple complex that attests to the central role of Hinduism and later Buddhism in what present-day country?	Cambodia
The CN Tower, one of the tallest structures in the world, offers excellent views of what nearby Great Lake from its observation decks?	Lake Ontario
The Collegiate Church of St. Peter at Westminster, popularly known as Westminster Abbey, and the adjacent Palace of Westminster are landmarks in what European capital city?	London
The Valley of the Kings and the Valley of the Queens, full of archeological treasures dating back to 1500 BC, are famous tourist attractions in which country?	Egypt
La Sagrada Família, a neo-Gothic cathedral designed by Catalan architect Antoni Gaudí dominates the skyline of what Mediterranean coast city in Spain?	Barcelona
Completed in 1967, Ostankino Tower is the tallest free standing structure in Europe. In what country is Ostankino Tower located?	Russia
Built by the Nabateans in the first century BC, the city of Petra is famous for rock-cut architecture carved from sandstone. What present-day country that borders Israel would you visit to see Petra?	Jordan
The Taj Mahal, regarded as one of the most beautiful buildings in the world, is on the southern banks of what river?	Yamuna River
The Doge's Palace and Piazza San Marco are two popular structures among tourists visiting which historic Italian city?	Venice

Question	Answer
Trafalgar Square is a popular tourist spot and is often the site of political demonstrations. Trafalgar Square is in the central part of what European capital city?	London
Our Lady of Peace of Yamoussoukro Basilica, considered to be the largest Christian church in the world, is in which African country?	Cote d'Ivoire
The Potala Palace, a treasure of Tibetan history, religion, and culture, is in which city?	Lhasa
What country would you visit to see the Sistine Chapel, which contains two of the world's most celebrated frescoes, *Genesis* and *The Last Judgment*?	Vatican City
Stonehenge, a prehistoric monument consisting of a circular group of large upright stones, is located in what plain in England?	Salisbury Plain
Built during the 12th century for King Suryavarman II, Angkor Wat is a renowned Hindu temple complex that attests to the central role of Hinduism and later Buddhism in what present-day country?	Cambodia
The CN Tower, one of the tallest structures in the world, offers excellent views of what nearby Great Lake from its observation decks?	Lake Ontario
10 Downing Street in the city of Westminster is one of the most famous addresses in which country—the U.K. or Canada?	the U.K.
The Collegiate Church of St. Peter at Westminster, popularly known as Westminster Abbey, and the adjacent Palace of Westminster are landmarks in what European capital city?	London
The Valley of the Kings and the Valley of the Queens, full of archeological treasures dating back to 1500 BC, are famous tourist attractions in which country?	Egypt
La Sagrada Família, a neo-Gothic cathedral designed by Catalan architect Antoni Gaudí dominates the skyline of what Mediterranean coast city in Spain?	Barcelona
Completed in 1967, Ostankino Tower is the tallest free standing structure in Europe. In what country is Ostankino Tower located?	Russia
Built by the Nabateans in the first century BC, the city of Petra is famous for rock-cut architecture carved from sandstone. What present-day country that borders Israel would you visit to see Petra?	Jordan
The Taj Mahal, regarded as one of the most beautiful buildings in the world, is on the southern banks of what river?	Yamuna River
The Doge's Palace and Piazza San Marco are two popular structures among tourists visiting which historic Italian city?	Venice

Question	Answer
The Leaning Tower of Pisa is located in the city of Pisa on the Arno River near the Ligurian Sea. Pisa is located in which Italian region?	Tuscany
Considered one of the Seven Wonders of the Ancient World, the Temple of Artemis at Ephesus is a popular tourist destination. What present-day, predominantly Muslim country would you visit to see this ancient wonder?	Turkey
The spectacular sea cliffs of Moher in County Clare rise to more than 600 feet above the Atlantic Ocean and are the most visited tourist attraction of what European Country?	Ireland

Question	Answer
Chapter 29. Regional and International Organizations	
The headquarters of the United Nations is located in which American city?	New York City
The Organization for Economic Co-operation and Development (OECD) was founded in 1961 to stimulate economic progress and commerce and had 33 member countries as of January 1, 2011. Most member countries of the OECD are in which continent?	Europe
The Association of Caribbean States promotes regional cooperation and integration among member countries. The secretariat of the organization is located in the city of Port of Spain in what country?	Trinidad and Tobago
Mercosur, a regional trade agreement among member countries, was founded in 1991 by the Treaty of Asunción. Mercosur was established to promote free trade among countries on which continent?	South America
In 1971, China replaced what country as a permanent member of the United Nation's Security Council?	Taiwan
Which country is not a member of the South Asian Association of Regional Cooperation—India, Afghanistan, or Myanmar?	Myanmar
OPEC, which is a cartel of countries from Asia, Africa, and South America, sets supply targets and seeks stabilization of prices in international oil markets. What does OPEC stand for?	Organization of the Petroleum Exporting Countries
Which two countries in the Western Hemisphere are members of NATO?	U.S.A. and Canada
The headquarters of the World Bank and the International Monetary Fund are located in which capital city?	Washington, D.C.
In 2004, Estonia, Latvia, and Lithuania became members of what defense alliance whose members include the U.S.A. and France?	NATO
The Organization of American States (OAS) is a regional organization of 35 countries in the Western Hemisphere and promotes peace and security. OAS' main building is located on the corner of 17th Street and Constitution Avenue in which capital city?	Washington, D.C.
The International Atomic Energy Agency (IAEA) promotes the peaceful use of nuclear energy among nations. IAEA headquarters are located in a European capital city where German is the official language. Name this capital city.	Vienna
Which country is not a member of the Association of Southeast Asian Nations—Indonesia, Taiwan, or Myanmar	Taiwan
The town of Davos, situated at an elevation of 5,000 feet in Graubünden Canton, hosts the annual meeting of the World Economic Forum every January. Davos is located in what landlocked European country?	Switzerland

Question	Answer
Which predominantly Muslim country has been a member of NATO since 1952?	Turkey
What international organization that promotes peace and security through education, science, and culture is headquartered in Paris?	UNESCO
The African Union, a pan-African organization which supports integration among its 53 member nations, is headquartered in the most populous city in the Horn of Africa. Name this city that is the world's largest city in a landlocked country.	Addis Ababa
As of January 2015, which country was not a member of the European Union—Bulgaria, Slovenia, or Norway?	Norway
The headquarters of the North Atlantic Treaty Organization (NATO) are located in which European city?	Brussels
The second most populous city in Switzerland, located between the Alps and the Jura Mountains at the extreme southwest corner of the country, is a global city and hosts more than 100 international organizations including the Red Cross, the World Health Organization (WHO), and the World Trade Organization (WTO). Name this city.	Geneva
The headquarters for the International Crop Research Institute for the Semi-Arid Tropics (ICRISAT) are located near a large city in the Deccan Plateau. Name this city where Telugu is widely spoken.	Hyderabad
The headquarters for the Asian Development Bank are located in what large city at the mouth of the Pasig River?	Manila
The headquarters of the Organization of Eastern Caribbean States are located in the city of Castries in which country?	Saint Lucia
Name the specialized agency of the United Nations located in Rome, Italy, that fights world hunger by raising nutritional levels and increasing agricultural productivity.	Food and Agriculture Organization
The International Olympic Committee, whose membership consists of 205 national Olympic committees, is based in which city that is the capital of Vaud Canton?	Lausanne
The general secretariat of Interpol, the international police organization for apprehending international criminals, is located in what city that is situated at the confluence of the Rhone and Saone Rivers?	Lyon

Question	Answer
Chapter 30. Civil Wars, Separatist Movements, and Disputes	
Possession of Siachen Glacier, which is located in the Kashmir region of Asia, is disputed between India and which other country?	Pakistan
ETA, the Basque nationalist and separatist organization fighting for a separate country, claims to represent all the Basques living in southwestern France and what other country?	Spain
Separatists in Chechnya, a region near the Caucasus ridge, are fighting for a separate country. Chechnya is in what country?	Russia
The Golan Heights, a strategic plateau and mountainous region, is being disputed by Israel and what other country?	Syria
Podgorica, formerly known as Titograd, is the capital of what country that acquired independence from Serbia in 2007?	Montenegro
Abkhazia and South Ossetia, two regions that border Russia along the Caucasus ridge, are fighting for independence from what country?	Georgia
The Tamil Tigers waged a violent secessionist campaign for a separate country for Tamil-speaking people in what island country?	Sri Lanka
The Potsdam Conference, a major post-World War II conference among the Allied Powers took place in July, 1945, in Cecilienhof Palace to negotiate terms for the end of World War II. Cecilienhof Palace is in which present-day country?	Germany
After a long and bloody struggle for self-determination, on February 17, 2008, this region, with ethnic Albanians making up 95 percent of its population, declared independence from Serbia. Name this region which is bordered by Montenegro and the Republic of Macedonia.	Kosovo
Brunei, China, Malaysia, the Philippines, Taiwan, and Vietnam all lay claim to the Spratly Islands. Although the total area of the islands does not exceed four square miles, the Spratly Islands are important for economic and strategic reasons. The Spratly Islands are located in what sea?	South China Sea
Tiny Migingo Island, located in the northeastern portion of Lake Victoria, is about the size of half a football field. Migingo Island is currently in dispute between Uganda and what other country?	Kenya
Syria, Iraq, and what other country have large numbers of Kurdish people seeking a separate country?	Turkey
The Ilemi Triangle, a small region in central Africa, is claimed by South Sudan, Kenya, and what other country?	Ethiopia
The high altitude Aksai Chin area, a part of the Tibetan Plateau that is controlled by China, is claimed by what neighboring country?	India

Question	Answer
Maidan Nezalezhnosti, known simply as Maidan, has been the traditional place for political rallies in the city Kiev. During November and December 2014, the Maidan witnessed large demonstrations demanding closer European integration and improved human rights. To which country would you go to visit the Maidan?	Ukraine
Ties between China and Japan have been strained by a territorial dispute over a group of tiny uninhabited islands known as the Senkaku Islands in Japan and the Diaoyu Islands in China. These islands are located in what body of water?	East China Sea
The Hala'ib Triangle, which is located on the Red Sea's African coast, is disputed between Egypt and what other country?	Sudan
What Mexican state that borders Guatemala witnessed an uprising of natives called Zapatistas in 1994?	Chiapas
The sovereignty of the southernmost Kuril Islands is under dispute by which two countries ?	Japan and Russia
What African country seeks to gain control of the Ceuta and Melilla exclaves of Spain?	Morocco
In mid-2010, protests between the ethnic Muslims and minority Christians in the city of Osh became violent. Osh, one of the oldest settlements in Central Asia, is the second largest city in which country?	Kyrgyzstan
The McMahon Line demarks the disputed border between India's Arunachal Pradesh and what other country?	China
All of the land west of the Essequibo River in Guyana is claimed by what other country?	Venezuela
The Sahrawi rebels of what disputed region in Saharan Africa claim a separate country by the name of Sahrawi Arab Democratic Republic?	Western Sahara
Name the largest but sparsely populated province in China where native Uyghur people are pressing for greater autonomy.	Xinjiang
Although not recognized as a separate country by the U.N., Transnistria or Transdniester unilaterally declared its independence from what country in 1990?	Moldova

Question	Answer
Chapter 31. Physical Geography	
Levees are often constructed to prevent what natural disaster—floods or earthquakes?	Floods
A seismograph is a device used for detecting the presence of what phenomenon?	Earthquake
What kind of rock is limestone—sedimentary or igneous?	Sedimentary
What trees are found in tidal flats, estuaries, and muddy coasts in tropical areas—mangrove or pine?	Mangrove
What is the name for an area within a desert region where there is sufficient water to sustain animal and plant life throughout the year?	Oasis
The point on the Earth's surface that is directly above the focus of an earthquake is called what?	Epicenter
What do you call a steep section of a river channel with turbulent high velocity flow?	Rapid
What term is used to describe the molten rock found below the Earth's crust?	Magma
What best describes an equinox—the precise point in time when the sun appears directly overhead at the equator or the point in time when the Earth is closest to the Sun?	Sun is directly over equator
A sea wave, with a long wavelength, generated by submarine earthquakes or volcanic activity is called what—a hurricane or tsunami?	Tsunami
What kind of lake is formed by a meandering river—an oxbow lake or alpine lake?	Oxbow lake
What term is used to refer to a portion of continental crust that extends out from the continent below the sea level—ionic crust or continental shelf?	Continental shelf
The portion of a river valley inundated by water during flooding is known as—a flood plain or water table?	Flood plain
Name the thick layer of the Earth's interior that lies between the crust and the core.	Mantle
Very little of the harmful ultraviolet energy from the Sun ever reaches the surface of the Earth because it is absorbed by what substance in the Earth's atmosphere—ozone or water vapor?	Ozone
The regular and predictable rise and fall of the water level of the Earth's oceans caused by the alignment of the Earth, Moon, and Sun is called what—flooding or tide?	Tide

Question	Answer
Riparian corridors are likely to occur near what physical forms—rivers or mountains?	Rivers
A flat-topped and often steep-sided hill standing isolated on a flat plain is referred to as—a butte or fjord?	Butte
What plants are more dominant in cool temperate climates with distinct seasons—evergreens or deciduous plants?	Deciduous plants
Which type of irrigation has the least water loss through evaporation—flood irrigation, sprinkler irrigation, or drip irrigation?	Drip irrigation
What technique do scientists use to approximate the age of fossilized remains of plants and animals—carbon dating or remote sensing?	Carbon dating
What is the term for the funnel-shaped depression at the summit of a volcano?	Crater
What word is used to describe the outermost layer of the solid Earth?	Crust
Where are you most likely to see a fjord—Norway, Panama, or Bangladesh?	Norway
Which river has a bigger delta—the Amazon or Mississippi River?	Amazon
What is a mesa—a steep sided plateau or a meandering river?	A steep sided plateau
Basal ice, a relatively thin layer of debris-rich ice, is found in what part of a glacier?	Base or bottom
What lines are used on a relief map to indicate points that have the same elevation—parallel lines, contour lines, or latitudes?	Contour lines
What term is used to describe a large mass of ice formed by the compaction and recrystallization of snow that moves very slowly downslope on land?	Glacier
The breakdown of rock material at or near the Earth's surface due to atmospheric exposure is called what—weathering or erosion?	Weathering
What do you call a rocky construction found at or near sea level formed mainly from biogenically produced carbonates?	Reef or bioherm
Which of the following is not a potential adverse consequence of prolonged excess irrigation—lowered water table, salinization, or forest fires?	Forest fires
What is observed in a layer of temperature inversion—an increase in temperature with altitude or a decrease in temperature with altitude?	Increase
The section of a river which flows into the sea where fresh and salt waters mix due to tidal currents is known by what term—estuary, headwaters, or tsunami?	Estuary

Question	Answer
What explains the formation of the Himalayan mountain range—collision of two continental plates or alternate freezing and thawing of glaciers?	Collision of two continental plates
The highly decomposed plant and animal residue that is a part of soil is known as—humus, silt, or loam?	Humus
The land area that contributes runoff to a stream is called its watershed or water table?	Watershed
An intense convectional storm associated with a cumulonimbus cloud is known by what name—thunderstorm or caldera?	Thunderstorm
The downward movement of earth or rock along slopes that is generally prompted by increased precipitation or snow melt is called what?	Landslide or landslip
The United Arab Emirates uses the process of desalination for producing what natural substance?	Fresh water
What is the term for the study of the relationship of plants and animals to their physical and biological environment?	Ecology
What energy is used by geographers for remote sensing—infrared or ultraviolet?	Infrared
The climate in Southern California, central Chile, and the South African coast near Cape Town that is characterized by hot dry summers and wet winters is known by what name associated with a body of water?	Mediterranean Climate
Rills are shallow channels that often form in sets on sloping agricultural lands and earthen embankments with no cover. Rills are caused by what agent—intense run-offs or intense winds?	Run-offs
What name is used for a zone located near the Equator that is characterized by low atmospheric pressure, high humidity, and frequent cloudy weather with light, variable winds—horse latitudes, pampas, or doldrums?	Doldrums
What term is used to describe the sections of the Earth's crust that move to cause continental drift and volcanic activity?	Tectonic plates
The Mohorovičić discontinuity, usually referred to as the Moho, is the boundary between the Earth's crust and what layer that lies below the crust?	Mantle
What is an important characteristic of anoxic water found deep in blue holes off the coast of the Bahamas—little dissolved oxygen or high iron content?	Little dissolved oxygen
The breaking away of a mass of ice from a floating glacier or ice shelf to form an iceberg or brash ice is known as what—calving, sublimation, or weathering?	Calving
The crust, the outermost layer of the Earth that runs about 5 to 25 miles in thickness, is generally thinner where—under the oceans or on the continents?	Under the oceans

Question	Answer
Willy-willies in Australia refer to what phenomenon—landslides, tropical cyclones, or earthquakes?	Tropical cyclones
A narrow, high-altitude, high-velocity stream of air that affects civilian aviation is known by what term—jet stream or wind turbulence?	Jet stream
A zone of increased air temperature usually associated with a large urban area is known as what—doldrums, heat island, or bajotermal?	Heat island
The acquisition of information such as temperature and moisture about objects from a distance without physical contact with those objects is called what—remote sensing or GPS?	Remote sensing
If you travel westward across the International Date Line do you advance your calendar day once or do you set back your calendar day once?	Advance
An intense low-latitude storm that typically brings with it both high winds and torrential rains is called what—tropical cyclone or doldrums?	Tropical cyclone
The subtropical latitudes near 30° S and 30° N which are marked by stable dry weather, high atmospheric pressure, and light winds are known by what term?	Horse latitudes
Which is an example of non-point source pollution—discharge from a chemical factory into a wash, discharge from a ship at sea, or leaching of excess fertilizer to groundwater?	Leaching of fertilizer to groundwater
A fjord, from Old Norse fjörthr, is best described as a narrow sea inlet extending deep into a steep cliffside. Are fjords more common in cold or warm climates?	Cold climates
The process by which snow or ice is lost from a glacier is known as what—ablation, dissolution, or expulsion?	Ablation
Large scale commercial production and use of CFCs by human beings in the 20th century is considered to have destroyed ozone in the Earth's stratosphere. CFC stand for what?	Chlorofluorocarbon
The scientific study of landforms and the processes that shape them is called—geomorphology or lechometrics?	Geomorphology
What are chotts found in North Africa—gusty winds, seasonal saline lakes, or short camels?	Seasonal saline lakes
What term, meaning "rock layer" in Greek, is used to describe the Earth's crust and the upper part of its mantle?	Lithosphere
What type of volcanoes do not erupt violently and are generally found at mid-ocean ridges or at hot spots in the sea?	Shield volcanoes

Question	Answer
The Palmer Index, which is measured on a scale of -4 to 4, takes into account precipitation, evapotranspiration, runoff, and soil moisture to assess the severity of what phenomenon?	Drought (or wetness)
A broad, shallow volcanic crater typically filled by a lake is known as what—maar or butte?	Maar
What term is used to describe a large roughly circular volcanic depression—mesa, caldera, or igneous crust?	Caldera
Explosive volcanoes that generally occur near plate boundaries where subduction is taking place are known as what type of volcanoes?	Stratovolcanoes
Xerophytes, plants that have adapted to harsh conditions by storing water and by developing abilities such as imbibing water from condensed atmospheric moisture, can be found in what country—Chile, Burundi, or Sri Lanka?	Chile
What is a limitation of Mercator projection, the most commonly used method for making maps that represent the Earth on a flat surface—exaggerating size of land areas near the poles, exaggerating the heights of mountain peaks, exaggerating the population of smaller countries?	Exaggerating size of land areas near the poles
What is the name of the cold ocean current that runs south from Greenland off the northeastern coast of Canada and brings nutrients and fog to the fishing grounds of the Grand Banks?	Labrador Current or Arctic Current
Which process can cause the formation of kettle lakes—prolonged rains, retreating glaciers, or meandering rivers?	Retreating glaciers
Which physical form is exposed to or contains saline water—playa or cienega?	Playa
Muskeg is a Canadian-Indian term used for describing what kind of land terrain—a bog formed by accumulation of moss or soil permanently frozen and covered by ice?	Bog
Flat-topped underwater mountains on the sea floor that are commonly found in the Pacific Ocean are known by what term—guyots or aquabuttes?	Guyots
What do you call a piece of floating sea ice which is not attached to land—ice cap, ice floe, or ice shelf?	Ice floe
What is a characteristic of katabatic winds—they move down slopes or they are more active on open seas?	Downslope winds
What kinds of plants are more dominant in high boreal forests—evergreens or deciduous trees?	Evergreens
What do dendroclimatologists study for making inferences about past climates—tree rings, volcanic deposits, or glacier patterns?	Tree rings

Question	Answer
Speleology is the scientific study of what physical forms—volcanoes, caves, or glaciers?	Caves
The northern part of the ancient supercontinent Pangaea is called—Laurasia or Gondwanaland?	Laurasia
What term is used to describe a deflecting force exerted on a parcel of air or any moving body due to the rotation of the Earth?	Coriolis force
A small volcanic vent through which acid gases are emitted, usually in areas where violent volcanism has ceased, is known by what term—solfatara, magma chamber, or humus escape?	Solfatara
A small sand dune or a mound formed when windblown sediment is trapped within or accumulates around a shrub is known as what—nebkha or dell?	Nebkha
The thick accumulations of bird excrement that are usually found on islands where birds nest are used as fertilizer for their richness in phosphorous. This bird excrement is known by what term—guano, biome, or manure?	Guano
Lichenometry is a method of establishing what aspect of a rock or deposit of glacial origin?	Age
Warm dry winds which blow down the eastern slopes of the Rocky Mountains of North America are known by what name?	Chinook
What term is used to describe the process in which one tectonic plate is forced deep into earth by its collision with another plate?	Subduction
Which clouds are lower—cirrus or cumulus?	Cumulus
The cold dry wind that blows southward in winter and spring affecting the Rhone Valley in southern France is known by what name?	Mistral
Which physical forms have fumaroles—deep valleys, mesas, or volcanoes?	Volcanoes
Inselbergs, Bornhardts, and Kopjes are all forms of what physical feature—glaciers, hills, or winds?	Hills
The Earth wobbles as it revolves in a way similar to that in which a top wobbles when spun. What is this wobble is called—precession, Coriolis force, or orbiteering?	Precession
The hot partially molten layer of the Earth's mantle that lies below the lithosphere is called by what word meaning "weak layer" in Greek?	Asthenosphere
What ocean current brings cold water to the southwest coast of Africa?	Benguela Current

Question	Answer
What word is used to describe easily worked fertile soil composed of clay, silt, and sand—loam, magma, or bog?	Loam
What term is used to refer to a mass of earth and rock debris carried by an advancing glacier and left behind as the glacier retreats?	Moraine
Under certain conditions, melted water at a glacier's surface and at the base of a sliding glacier refreezes. What term is used to describe this refreezing of melted water?	Regelation
The downward movement of water through soil which results in the removal of water-soluble minerals from the upper layers and their accumulation in groundwater or a lower soil zone is called what?	Leaching
Which of these lines on a map is not an isopleth—a line connecting points of equal snow depth, a line connecting points of equal rainfall, or a line connecting fresh water lakes?	Line connecting fresh water lakes
What term is used for circular, steep-walled underwater sinkholes or submarine vertical caves found off the coasts of the Bahamas and Belize?	Blue holes
The addition of mineral nutrients such as nitrogen and phosphorous to lakes by farm runoffs is an example of what process—erosion, eutrophication, or veering?	Eutrophication
Etesian winds, whose name is derived from the Greek word *etesios*, meaning annual, blow steadily from the north bringing cold continental air during the summer over which sea?	Aegean Sea
An earthquake measuring 6 on the Richter scale is how many times more powerful than one measuring 4?	100 times
Lithification is a process by which loose sediments are converted into what objects?	Rocks
Which of these is a cold wind—Santa Ana, Brickfielder, or Bora?	Bora
What term is used for a vertical cylindrical shaft or hole in a glacier into which surface meltwater flows?	Moulin or glacier mill
The processes of retrogradation and progradation occur at which end of the river—headwaters or mouth?	Mouth
Fluvial deposits are made by which physical form—rivers or retreating glaciers?	Rivers
What is the Lomonosov Ridge—an underwater ridge in the Arctic Ocean or a ridge in Norway?	Underwater ridge in Arctic Ocean
A saline flat or depression that is subject to occasional inundation by sea water is known by what Arabic word—moraine, sabkha, or solfatara?	Sabkha

Question	Answer
The deposits from streams that flow subglacially are known to form curvy ridges of gravel that are many miles in length and several hundred feet in height. These ridges are known by what term?	Eskers
Scientists install stilling wells at the edge of a river channel or in a river bank for measuring what—total precipitation, river levels, or evapotranspiration?	River levels
Fossilized animal dung or excrement is important for archeologists for making inferences about the diet and behavior of prehistoric animals. What word of Greek origin, meaning dung stone, is used to describe fossilized animal dung?	Coprolite
In meteorology, an okta is a measure of the amount of what?	Cloud cover
What word of German origin is used to describe a warm dry wind that descends usually at high speed on the leeward side of a mountain range, especially the Alps?	Foehn [*fayn*]
What is the name for the ancient sea that is thought to have separated Laurasia and Gondwanaland?	Tethys Ocean
Arrange these sediments by particle size from the largest to the smallest—clay, silt, and sand.	Sand, silt, clay
Clusters of elongated oval- or tear-shaped hills formed by a moving glacier are known by what word of Gaelic origin—dell, fjord, or drumlin?	Drumlin
A sverdrup (Sv), named in honor of the Norwegian oceanographer, is a unit for measuring what aspect of ocean currents?	Measure of volume transport. 1 Sv = 1 million cubic meters per second
Currently the Earth's axis is tilted 23.5 degrees. Because the Earth wobbles as it rotates and revolves around the Sun, the tilt of earth's axis varies from 21.5 to 24.5 degrees over a period of about 40,000 years. This variation in axial tilt is called what?	Nutation
Moder, mor, and mull are three forms of what substance in soil?	Organic matter or humus
What is the Icelandic term that geographers use for catastrophic floods from a subglacial or ice-dammed lake?	Jökulhlaup